About the Author

John Holmstrom is an award-winning writer, producer, director, and cameraman. He has traveled and/or filmed in the U.S. and over forty countries while involved in the production of TV documentaries, commercials, sports, travel, industrial films and videos, and a feature film.

In 1986, he was commissioned to document and videotape individuals who had been healed of physical and personal problems through prayer. This experience gave Holmstrom the impetus to rely on prayer to overcome his own addiction to alcohol.

While producing and writing films, Holmstrom has interviewed witch doctors in Africa, Sioux medicine men, race car drivers, actors, athletes, refugees, the homeless, and many others. His writing and still photography have appeared in the *Detroit News*, *Pageant* magazine, *Christian Science Monitor*, and *American Cinematographer*.

When Prayers Are Answered

John Holmstrom

A Perigee Book

The song lyrics on page 164 are taken from "On Eagles' Wings" by Michael Jones, copyright © 1979 New Dawn Music, 5536 NE Hassalo, Portland, OR 97213. All rights reserved. Used by permission.

A Perigee Book
Published by The Berkley Publishing Group
200 Madison Avenue
New York, NY 10016

Book design by Joseph Perez
Cover design by James R. Harris

First edition: October 1995

Published simultaneously in Canada.

Library of Congress Cataloging-in-Publication Data
Holmstrom, John.
When prayers are answered / John Holmstrom.—1st ed.
p. cm.
"A Perigee book."
ISBN 0-399-52159-3 (pbk.)
1. Prayer—Christianity. I. Title.
BV210.2.H66 1995
248.2'2—dc20 95–7695
CIP

Printed in the United States of America

10 9 8 7 6 5 4 3 2 1

This book is gratefully dedicated to the memory of my mother and father, who planted its seed within me as a child, and to all those who seek to separate the tares from the wheat.

Acknowledgments

In November of 1992 I conducted my first interview for this book; my final one was in January of 1995. In between those dates I received encouragement and help from numerous people. My brothers, Peter and David, my dear stepmother, Melba, my sister-in-law Patricia, and my nieces Krista and Laurel were particularly supportive and loving during the months I devoted to the writing of this book.

I thank you all for patiently listening to my problems, reading some of my rough drafts and enduring my endless stories about my various adventures while traveling through the U.S.

Longtime friends, acquaintances, and people I only talked to on the phone helped me locate the individuals I interviewed. I was also given invaluable advice and insights regarding the publishing world from various people. Without this unselfish help, my task in researching and writing this book would have been even more formidable. I gratefully acknowledge all their contributions and encouragement: Keith Atkinson, Jim Bencivanga, Pam and Nate Benjamin, Bruce Bryant, Lynne Bundesen, Landt and Lisl Dennis, Fred C. Dobbs, Junie Donleavey, Cindy Doyle, Nathalie DuPree, Chris Ellinshaw, Rob Gilbert, Rita Henniger, Kathi Henry, Betsy Hutchinson, Brian Kennedy, Karen Lanza, Lonnie Lardner, Rosemary

Layng, Pamela Lishin, Barbara Logan, Walter Matthews, Dr. Blaine Mays, Jim McMullan, Bob Moline, Delores Patch, Glen Peters, Quinn Redeker, Wendy Remington, Lissa Layng Reynolds, Jean Stine, Wintress Strong, Christine Tomovich, Julia Wade, and a very special thanks to Jennifer Essen for her thoughtful insight and suggestions.

I'm also grateful for Meredith Babeaux Brucker, a former Monrovia, California, High School classmate and present-day author and writing teacher, who reappeared in my life to graciously advise and assist me when I needed it.

To Jeff Herman and Debra Adams of the Jeff Herman Agency I owe thanks for bringing this book to my publisher and eventually to my editor, Julie Merberg, and her assistant, Hardy Justice. Their patience and razor-sharp editing considerably improved and focused my writing efforts and were immensely appreciated, as was Donna Gould for her enthusiastic and well-organized promotional campaign.

I talked to seventy or eighty people while researching interviews for this book. I'm sorry they weren't all included, but I feel the stories presented here best represent the book's purpose: to explore why people pray, how they pray, and the result.

I did a lot of praying during the two-year process of writing this book, which included researching, finding an agent and a publisher, traveling by car and airplane across the U.S. to interview my subjects, transcribing the interviews, writing and rewriting the chapters, as well as photographing some of the people. My prayers were definitely answered as I was led to a wide variety of wonderful people who unselfishly discussed their prayer experiences with me. I humbly thank you all for allowing me to share your unique stories with my readers.

Introduction

W*hen Prayers Are Answered* is a book about ordinary people who talk about their often life-threatening problems—and how they turned to prayer for help. Hopefully, their stories will initiate within your thinking—regardless of your prayer beliefs—an awareness of, if not an appreciation for, the power of prayer.

Their experiences are as different as one could expect in a country with approximately 1600 religions. Understanding prayer, let alone the spiritual forces attendant to it, is elusive because we seek its meaning through human concepts instead of divine.

Can prayer bridge this gap between the human and the divine? Based on my own experience and the ones in this book, I'd say yes. Consider the problems overcome through prayer in this book: alcoholism, cancer, multiple sclerosis, adultery, broken bones, drug addiction, fear, smoking, lupus, and abuse.

Why does prayer work for some and not others? I don't really know. But my prayer experiences and the catharsis of writing this book have prodded me along a spiritual path that perhaps someday will provide me with an answer to this age-old question.

I first became aware of the power of prayer when I was a nineteen-year-old soldier in the Army in Okinawa. While swimming in the ocean, strong winds signaling the advent of a typhoon swept across the beach. Afraid to return to the base, I huddled by a rock for shelter. Unexpectedly, the wind died down so I returned to camp. Within hours the full force of the typhoon hit the island but I was safe in the barracks.

A letter from my mother and a later discussion with her indicated that at the time I was trapped on the beach, she awoke at night in California and told my dad that they should pray for me, which they did.

Later, while attending college, I was bedridden with a migraine headache. My dear father sat with me, held my head and prayed. In minutes I was asleep and when I awoke I was well.

In 1975, I was producing a film in Detroit when my brother Peter phoned my hotel at night from California to tell me that our mother had passed away. It was not unexpected, as she had been ill, but I loved her very much and I lay on my bed, tears filling my eyes. Suddenly, in the darkness, I saw my mother standing next to the bed. She said very clearly, "Don't cry, John. I'm not dead. I haven't died."

Had I imagined this, was I dreaming, did my grief produce what I wanted to see and hear . . . ? (I later learned my father also had the same experience with my mother after her passing.)

Although grateful for these unique experiences, I was the recipient of my parents' spiritual understanding, not my own; I believed in prayer but I made no real effort to comprehend it.

This all changed in 1986 when my own prayers were answered.

As a documentary filmmaker with twenty years of international experience, I had gradually slipped into drinking to excess four to five times a week. I was also unemployed, had broken up with a girlfriend, a business partnership had ended and I had lost the majority of my savings because a "financial advisor" gave me very bad advice. In the midst of these problems and my resultant self-pity and depression, it was easier to drink than to face and solve all my difficulties.

In mid-1986, during all of my problems, I was hired to shoot a video about prayer for the First Church of Christ Scientist in Boston. In the past, my career as a producer and director involved me in films on the African famine; self-help programs in Bangladesh, Honduras and Thailand; a film on the miracle of Fatima in Portugal; and a film for the Navajo Tribe. Filming deeply religious people was not new to me.

However, this time, as I shot at locations in the U.S. and overseas, I listened with great interest to the people being interviewed—including someone who'd been healed of alcoholism—as they discussed their prayer experiences. I'd been raised in a very happy family by loving, religious parents, but God and prayer was never really discussed in a way that I could relate to.

After the month of filming, I realized that I must stop drinking through prayer, not self-will. I'd quit drinking many times, often for several months, but inevitably I'd return to the habit.

So I prayed, not to humanly stop drinking, but to acknowledge my growing belief that as a child of God I was born in His image and likeness, hence I wasn't an alcoholic or depressed because God wasn't. I began to believe in my own spirituality and my continual prayers celebrated that.

A month later, I left a supermarket without buying any

alcohol, a purchase I always made when shopping. I had no liquor in the house, but strangely, I didn't feel any urge to drink, a new experience for me. Later, I returned to the market and deliberately walked through the liquor department. I felt nothing. Three days later it dawned on me that my prayers had been answered. I haven't had a drink since then nor have I any interest in it.

During the next three or four years, I heard and read about many unique prayer experiences. I started a file of clippings and notes which soon filled a box. Although I've written scripts for some of my films, I never considered writing a book about prayer. But the idea grew in my thoughts, and in November 1992 I did my first interview for this book.

I wrote letters and made numerous phone calls while contacting religious groups, churches, synagogues, twelve-step programs and friends in search of subjects. Unfortunately, some whom I had hoped to include in the book never responded.

During my travels in eleven states I met some unique people, including Raphael Abiem, a soft-spoken Dinka tribesman from Sudan, Africa, at Harvard. He told me that although he was a divinity student, he didn't believe in prayer. "My prayer, God help me, is a waste because if God is infinite how can I expect to know more than God?" he declared. "I am here to be taken care of by God. Does my reminding him change anything? My praying creates the sphere of God and doer, and the sphere of me, the receiver. There cannot be a duality if God is infinite."

Raphael's fellow student Teresa Yugar enthusiastically told me a different story.

"Prayer is important because it helps to ground me, enables me to say 'This is why I'm here.' It's the way I connect with the divine. Prayer is a presence within me yet it embraces me."

Julia Penrose told about how a friend's car was stolen in Philadelphia, so she prayed and sang a hymn she'd learned in Sunday School, "Shepherd, Show Me How to Go." Six hours later, driving her own car on the other side of town, she discovered her friend's car abandoned and undamaged.

"The infinite Mind, God, knows everything. If you tune into that Mind, then you can find anything," she explained.

Muslim Esmerald Alfi from Pasadena, California, told me she successfully prayed to be free of cigarettes. "When I wanted to smoke I would sit and shake my head and body and pray, 'There is no God but Allah,' for twenty-five minutes until I got over the desire. In that emotional way of asking God's support, I made a covenant with Him."

At New York City's Buddhist Church, Dimitri Bakhroushin, a man who became interested in Buddhism while a soldier in Vietnam, said that he meditates rather than prays; "The relationship of meditation to prayer is the relationship between the canvas and the picture. A person who prays puts something on the canvas. Meditation prepares the canvas to be as receptive as possible."

I not only went to a Buddhist Church, I witnessed prayers at a Muslim Mosque, and at a Jewish Kabbalah Synagogue where I wore a yamulka and a prayer shawl while a man next to me explained the Hebrew service. I also visited Episcopal, Catholic, Christian Science, Methodist, Baptist, Jewish Science, and Self Realization Fellowship services, plus a Bible study class in a Federal prison, a Gamblers Anonymous meeting in Las Vegas, a singles group at a Hebrew University, an incest survivors talk, and an International New Thought Alliance convention in Texas.

Occasionally I was surprised. At a large Boston church the minister told me, "I don't know anyone that has had a healing or an unusual prayer experience in the congregation, but I'd be glad to talk to you about prayer."

That was in sharp contrast with the story of Pamela Curran, a woman from Boston who attended a Catholic healing service and was healed of her drug and alcohol addictions when a praying priest touched her. She said, "It was like a bolt of electricity shooting through me. I fell down and cried. Now, every morning I look in the mirror and say, 'You're glowing, kid!' And it's not a mescaline glow or a cocaine glow: It's a God glow."

People in the book discussed prayer in a variety of ways. Former nun Meinrad Craighead told me, "There is no prayer without listening because listening is having your ear cocked to the rhythms, sounds, forces, and energies of the universe. That's where God is."

Native American J. T. Garrett explained that "Prayer is an everyday part of Indian life. We don't segregate it into time frames or occasions or rituals. It's a way of life."

Jane Hingert-Eiduson, who was healed of lupus, told me, "When I pray it's informal, an aligning of my thought with the way God meant life to be for me, harmonious and joyful. I pray daily to know there's a loving God controlling everything, including me. From that I think all healing flows."

Janet Steele said, "I'm getting closer to God when I pray.

God doesn't have to be reminded that we exist. We have to be reminded that *He* exists!"

I often felt as if I was living in two worlds while writing this book. On one hand I interviewed people who had faced life-threatening problems. Prayer resolved their situations and changed their thinking and their lives.

But the world of TV, movies, newspapers and magazines that permeates our lives so often glorifies violence, power, sensuality, and money. I often became upset after an interview about a life-changing prayer experience when I realized how the world is increasingly programmed to view disaster, agony, and violence as entertainment.

Why are we so easily distracted from learning about our spirituality? Are we paying a price for media distortions and a microwave culture of fast foods, quickie divorces, instant car lubes, and one-hour photos? What do we do with this time we "save"?

During my travels I talked to a very spiritual woman about this dichotomy. She said, "People spend hours watching TV and movies, reading novels, going to school, working, and taking vacations. They often claim their parents' religion without examining their beliefs. They may spend an hour a week at church or praying. And then *Bam!* some calamity hits them. Then they pray. You wouldn't spend an hour a week studying law and expect to pass the bar exam, would you?"

Joyce Milgaard, who prayed for her son who was wrongly imprisoned for twenty-two years, gave a good analogy of the "two worlds" that confronted her when she asked, "God, what are you seeing? What's the truth here? It reminded me that when I saw a beautifully embroidered rose, the reverse was a tangle of knots. I felt my life was a tangle but I knew that God was seeing the perfection, the beauty of the finished rose."

In spite of all the turmoil in the world and the media's false images, I believe there is more love and compassion in the world than hate and violence. I think the people in this book are the emerging tip of a spiritual force of people who are confident that they can change lives and the world through prayer.

• • •

In July 1994, I stayed the night in an El Paso, Texas, motel after driving all day. During the drive I expressed my gratitude to God—which I believe is an important part of prayer—for a safe, problem-free trip, for the people I was being led to interview and for the love I felt He was pouring out to me while I was traveling.

I set my alarm for 5 A.M. as I had to be in Albuquerque, New Mexico, the next morning for an interview. Later, I was awakened by someone shaking my shoulder. I was startled since I was alone so I turned on the light. My clock said 5:15 A.M. and I discovered the alarm hadn't gone off because I had set it incorrectly. Who or what woke me up? Was I dreaming, did I imagine it . . . ?

Laurance Doyle, a Sunday school–teaching astrophysicist, gave me an insight about the power of prayer. He said, "We are on the verge of being forced by physics into accepting the fact that thought and body cannot be separated. What are the laws of thought? What are the laws of mind? That's the renaissance. That's what is coming. And that's why I pray."

When Prayers Are Answered

pray *(vb)* 1: to make entreaty or supplication 2: to address God with adoration, confession, supplication, or thanksgiving

—*Webster's Dictionary*

A Technicolor Life

Revelation when genuine is simply the record of the immediate experience of those who are pure enough in heart and poor enough in spirit to be able to see God.

Aldous Huxley

Mary Habel Chilton is a 52-year-old student at The General Theological Seminary in New York City. She and her husband, Hunter, an engineer, have two children and two grandchildren and a home in Rome, New York. Her grandfather was a Baptist minister, as were two of her father's brothers.

I interviewed Mary in her small, comfortably furnished apartment on the spacious seminary grounds. She was dressed simply and expressed a quiet air of purpose and spirituality. Mary has a doctorate in education, a master's in personnel management, and is a registered nurse. Before I began the interview we took a short walk on the seminary grounds and then visited the seminary's beautiful Chapel of the Good Shepherd.

In 1965 three different neurologists diagnosed me as having multiple sclerosis. I was 23, married with two children, and I was having trouble walking, speaking, and seeing.

My life became totally focused on the disease. We bought a home that was arranged so that if eventually I had to be in a wheelchair, it was possible. Though the M.S. didn't get worse over the years, I never knew when I would have an attack. I struggled with fatigue which caused an underlying depression in me. Living with M.S. was like having an albatross around my neck.

• • •

I grew up in a very religious home in the little Virginia town of Bentonville. I had an innocent childlike faith that was nurtured by a loving family and the Baptist church I went to.

When I went to college, I left that behind. Being a good southern Baptist, I was told never to date a Catholic, so of course the first thing I did when I hit campus was to find a Catholic boy to date. I'd never tasted alcohol, but I soon learned to enjoy a bourbon and coke. When I was almost 21, I got married. My husband, Hunter, and I didn't attend any church until our first child was born. Then we started attending the Presbyterian Church, which he had been brought up in.

When I was diagnosed with M.S. I remember trying to get close to God. I read the Scriptures but I couldn't make any connection with God. As an adult I had lost that childlike faith that previously had nurtured me. Part of the problem with my life was the disease—and the disease was always there. I couldn't escape from it, even when I read the Bible.

In 1975 a friend asked me to visit a Presbyterian minister who supposedly had the gift of healing. I told her I didn't believe in that kind of thing. I had trouble accepting healing because I was much too logical to be interested in any of this full gospel, laying-on-of-hands stuff. But my friend persisted. "You should go and have this man pray for you." I was scheduled to go to a Boston clinic for three days of neurological tests the next week, so I thought it probably wouldn't hurt to go see the minister first.

The prayer service was held in a church basement in the afternoon. The room had big windows, lots of light, and was quite pleasant. The minister was a benevolent man who conducted a short Bible study class. There were about ten or twelve middle-aged women in the group, with my friend and I being the youngest.

After the Bible study was over, the minister and the women came over to my chair and laid their hands on my shoulders and arms. A few put their hands on the person in front of them as they quietly grouped around me. Everyone was very loving and sincere. The minister prayed a simple prayer. He didn't mention my M.S., he just prayed for a healing. It wasn't a charismatic kind of prayer and it wasn't spoken in tongues. It was so simple I can't even remember what he said.

The prayer was only a few minutes long and when it was over, there was no warm feeling, no thunderclap, nothing at all. I kept thinking I'd feel something more, but I didn't feel any different physically or emotionally. But I thanked my friend for bringing me to the meeting and that was it.

The next day I went to the Boston clinic for three days of neurological tests. I was shocked to learn that the results indicated there was nothing wrong with me.

I literally flipped out. I screamed at my doctor, "What do you mean, there's nothing wrong with me? What's been going on for the past ten years? I've been to all these neurologists and now you're saying there's nothing wrong with me!"

Then I heard a voice—it wasn't audible to others; it was inside—telling me, "You've got a choice, Mary. You can take up your bed and walk or you can choose to remain on the mat."

Immediately, I thought of Jesus when he spoke to the man at the pool of Bethesda and told him to take up his bed and walk (John 5: 1-15). It really hit me. Did I want to be well? If so, I couldn't say I was too tired to do things. I'd now have to take responsibility for my own life again.

So I joined the Y, began to work out, and never looked back. After the doctors confirmed that nothing was wrong with me, I never returned to them. Doubters can say my M.S. is in remission, but I'm a registered nurse and I know it doesn't go into a twenty-year remission. Those tests were done in 1975, and it's now 1995. In that time I've never been hospitalized, nor do I take any medication. I'm as healthy as a person could be.

• • •

Even though my life had radically changed and my body was healthy, I went into a serious depression at first. I had been sick for so long, I didn't know how to be well. My family saw me as sick and I saw myself as sick, and then my world turned upside down when I was pronounced well. I went to a counselor for six months, and basically what I learned was that the responsibility for my life was on me.

During this time I'd been attending college. I received my master's and I started teaching part-time. But after my healing I felt I had to quit the job, as I was pinning my identity on it. The moment I quit, something happened that's hard to describe.

I went to a little Christian bookstore with my Bible in hand and said to the youth behind the counter, "This book is either real or it isn't, right? I'm going to find out if this is all real."

The young man was only 19 or 20, but he was in shock. It turned out he was a full gospel person and he probably thought, oh, boy, have I got a soul to save here! He invited me to his church and said they would pray for me so I would better understand the Bible.

"There is nothing written in here that says I have to go to a particular denomination. Why don't you pray for me right now?" I suggested. So he did.

Within a few weeks, my husband started saying, "What's happened to you, Mary? You're singing. What's going on in your life?" I realized that something had happened in my life because I felt a joy I'd never known and I couldn't devour enough of the Scriptures. I read them morning, noon, and night.

One night, about a month after my visit to the bookstore, I got down on my knees and said, "Okay, Lord. Give it to me." And then I began to speak in a language that was unknown to me. I was totally conscious of what was happening, but I didn't know what it was, and I thought "My God—What is this? It's really weird."

There was a girl living across the street who was a charismatic (Evangelical) Catholic so I ran to her house and asked her if I'd been speaking in tongues. She said yes, she too had spoken in tongues, and she knew that's what I was experiencing.

Several months later, Hunter also received the gift

of tongues. We often pray together and through our shared prayers, we have developed a sensitivity to the spirit. In a way, it's like returning to the trust you have in God as a child. We pray and listen to God and don't doubt His power.

As an example, one morning I had this tremendous urge to pray for Hunter, so I did. Later on he told me he'd been driving on slippery pavement when his car spun out of control—then suddenly he'd felt something surround the car and correct it. We discovered this had happened at the time I began praying for him. That's the kind of thing that has become a regular part of our lives.

• • •

I now realize that my healing has come in stages. The first stage was physical and very dramatic. But the emotional and spiritual healing I've experienced has been the most rewarding. The wholeness I feel now is incredible; it's as if God has put my life back together. I was expecting a revolution, but it was really an evolution. I turned over the barriers in my life when I surrendered them to Jesus Christ.

I keep a prayer journal with a list of people I pray for every night. I also mark down how my prayers are answered. I think God answers all of my prayers, but some answers are more evident than others.

I expect the unexpected when I pray. For example, our family was visiting the northern rim of the Grand Canyon recently and we discovered camping wasn't the best idea for my elderly mother-in-law, so we put our name on a waiting list for lodging in a cabin for her. But there were 11 people ahead of us. I prayed very specifically: "God, you know that she needs this room because she needs privacy and she's tired. Please, help us."

That evening, the lodging official announced that there were only a few rooms available, and we knew Mother was way down on the list. But the man read off one name, then skipped right down to hers, and she got a room. My husband was standing right there and saw it happen. God does answer very specific prayers.

Experiences like this increase my faith in God and the belief that He answers prayer. "Though you walk through the fire I will be with you." There is a tremendous power that emanates from God, and it's there for healing. Unfortunately most of us approach life trying everything before we try God.

In 1991 I enrolled in New York City's General Theological Seminary to become an Episcopal priest. After graduation I'll be running an outreach AIDS Shanti and an urban ministry for a church in Utica, New York. "Shanti" is Indian for "safe haven." It's one of those God-ordained jobs that I never would have asked for or sought. But now everything I have learned in my life will come together for this job.

I'm a registered nurse and I'll be working with AIDS patients. I have a doctorate in adult education and I'll be working with volunteers. And my master's in personnel management will help me run the Shanti. I've also been a prison volunteer for two years. I think it's been planned all my life to plunk me in this job.

My spiritual path has been one of growth through prayer and working through things—like the healing of M.S. and the depression I went through afterwards. I believe that overcoming all these challenges led me back to that simple, childlike faith I had in God and prayer when I was a child.

I see myself becoming more and more the person God intends me to be, using the talents and gifts He has given me. Attending seminary and becoming a priest is what I'm supposed to do. There is now a fullness and an enjoyment in life. If my life used to be black and white, now it's technicolor.

The Agony of an Artist

God is really only another artist. He invented the giraffe, the elephant, and the cat. He has no real style, He just goes on trying other things.

Pablo Picasso

Jonathan Rogers is a six-foot-one, rail-thin artist who lives in the small town of Lewiston, New York, with his fiancée, Alexandra, and their two cats. In their comfortable apartment, Jonathan, a good-humored and thoughtful man, is surrounded by the tools of his trade: brushes, paint, paper, and mounted and framed examples of his efforts as a painter and sketch artist. Canadian-born Jonathan is a jogger and a health-food devotee; a father of Naomi, 33, and Ben, 31; a grandfather; and a survivor of childhood sexual abuse.

Since 1984 I've been a friend of Jonathan's. I was unaware of his personal turmoil until a I shot a video of him participating in a sexual abuse survivors group in 1992.

I've had a ridiculous life with lots of ups and downs like a yo-yo. My mother was a sexual abuse victim, but it wasn't until I understood the symptoms that I could see where she was coming from. All I knew as a child was it was a compulsion with her to abuse her son. She just had to penetrate my body with things.

It doesn't make sense to give a kid an enema four or five times a day for days and days and years and years. I suffered a lot of anal penetration and I was often locked in a dark closet for extended periods of time during which she'd feed me but deprive me of all light. It was punishment or torture, of course, but my parents termed it "character building." Building my character became their obsession. I lived in constant fear of the next enema.

My Dad was also a tortured man, an alcoholic and an elder in the church. The churches we went to appeared to be very conventional. My parents got dressed up every Sunday and went to church, and I went to Sunday school.

Then in my teens I began to get interested in religion in a bigger way and began examining philosophies like Scientology, spiritualism, born-again Christianity, Buddhism, and anything that caught my interest. But over the years I gave up on everything I tried, including therapy.

I was seventeen when my Dad died, and I had had enough of my mother, so in 1956 I took off for four years by myself. I traveled through Canada, Alaska, Europe, North Africa, and the Middle East, on the go all the time.

In 1960 I met my wife in England, and we got married and had our son and daughter there.

I've always tried to earn my living as an artist because that's my main aptitude. But as many artists discover, it's hard to earn a livelihood doing what you love.

So at various times, I also worked in advertising, freelance photography, illustration, and fine arts, as well as portrait painting to make money. But instead of building on my success, I'd always find myself in a downward spiral until I lost everything. Then I'd get depressed, and beat myself up psychologically. I really believed I wasn't fit to be alive.

We moved thirteen times in thirteen years, during which time my family suffered terribly. Moving like that is very disruptive on kids, to say nothing of my wife, who was trying to be a mother, a homemaker, and a wife. I was out of control until 1980 or so, borrowing money, spending money, doing extravagant things. I was always drinking and smoking pot. For a long time, my wife had extraordinary patience and a lot of love, but she finally said, "Let me out. I've had it."

After my marriage broke up I got involved with a woman who was a survivor of incest and satanic cult abuse. When that relationship came to its inevitable disastrous end, all my resources were depleted. I was on welfare. I came down with pneumonia twice and I was going crazy. I had yet another business failure that wiped me out financially. I began to realize my life was going to be one catastrophe, one failure after another.

I'd always been suicidal, and I've owned a .32 revolver since I was nine years old. Carrying the gun meant I always had a way of killing myself, but it actually kept me from suicide: Whenever I'd pick up the gun to use it, the drama of the act would obscure the reason I wanted to kill myself, so I'd just put it away and get on with some other madness.

I went into about a year of dysfunctionality in 1991 when I was perpetually exhausted and I couldn't sleep, eat, or use the phone. I was a mess. I was doing some reading and talking with people and I slowly began to realize that we have a propensity to be attracted to the kind of people that we are. If I was so compulsively drawn in to being with a survivor of satanic cult abuse, what was it in my life that made me susceptible to all the problems I'd had?

I started going to two or three twelve-step recovery meetings for survivors of sexual abuse every week. The process of going to those meetings and delving into one's own problems started my learning process. Eventually it occurred to me that people everywhere seem to recognize a spiritual power. Through all their idols, totem poles, cathedrals, temples, all the symbolism and trappings, priests, and priestesses—it doesn't matter what culture you look at—all evidence this phenomenon of a higher power. This realization forced me to acknowledge that there just might be some invisible power. And I had nothing to lose by taking a trial run at it, assuming that if there was a power there, I could turn my life and will over to that power. So in November 1991, rather tentatively, but genuinely, I decided to surrender myself to that nameless higher power. I released all fears and trusted that someone, something would guide me. This act of faith was a very affirming, hopeful, powerful thing to do. It took all the nerve I've ever had.

• • •

I didn't immediately start to pray when I decided to turn my life over to a higher power, but eventually I thought it would be a good idea to try praying a few times a day.

Now I pray, I get down on my knees. It's a very appropriate physical position, because it's humbling and you find out if you're really sincere. I don't follow any formula except to declare that it is a prayer directed to a higher power. I've addressed that power as holy spirit, divine intelligence, divine consciousness, infinite being, great power, and I've even used the "G" word. *Almighty God!* That's an awesome term, isn't it? I don't detect any specific being or entity, gender, no father or mother, no goddess, no man up in the clouds. It's more of a spiritual current. As long as we're not in accord with this force, and not plugged into it, life is very difficult.

When I pray, I just say what's on my mind and what I feel. I don't light candles or have a liturgy. I just ask for answers and I get them, sometimes vividly, sometimes in words, sometimes in a dramatized sort of an experience that comes in a flash. I've never said the same prayer twice. Each prayer grows out of the circumstances I'm in. Praying is sort of like coming home for me. My only regret is that I didn't start doing it fifty-six years ago!

So my prayer is a prayer for guidance and "thy will be done" to be revealed to me. I live in a different mode than I've ever before lived in since I made the decision to believe. I pray night and day and in between when I need to. It's as though I've been lifted up into a higher experience. Things work out in ways that I cannot control or envision or hope. They just work out in the most unexpectedly beneficial ways.

• • •

All my life I'd had a lot of physical ailments, such as spastic colon and chronic intestinal pain and cramping. Those symptoms were the same ones I'd suffered as a child from the abuse by my mother. I've medicated myself with hundreds of medicines: suppositories, creams, ointments, lotions, pills and syrups—all to no avail. The first thing I noticed after I began praying was that the symptoms and the pain of all those lifelong conditions just vanished! For weeks and months afterwards, I was so impressed: When you live with a physical condition all your life and then it suddenly goes away, it's astounding!

My physical healing was only a part of my transformation, though. Shortly after my initial decision to turn my life over to a higher being, I had a vision that was unusually vivid, very clear, and it took me about an hour to draw it. It was a picture of a man who could have been a deity or god. He looked a little like me, though I didn't have that intent when I was drawing. (I didn't have any intent: I just drew.) The man was holding a very small, fetal-sized baby. The drawing—and the act of creating it—gave me a great feeling of healing, acceptance, and coming alive. I'd never drawn anything like this before; it was kind of corny and soft. It wasn't tough, macho or even "painterly."

But I really loved the picture, so I took it to a twelve-step meeting and showed it to various people in the group. A few cried when they saw it! In all my life as an artist, I've never had people cry over a drawing. It blew me away, so I made some prints and was going to give them away, but people insisted on paying me. I desperately needed the money, as I was seven months behind in the rent and owed $2500 in phone bills. I turned it over to a higher power and I did what I was guided to do; I drew more prints.

Soon afterwards, another child-abuse survivor in one of the groups proposed that he put up money to become partners with me to sell the prints commercially.

I did 25 more drawings over three months, and it was all so effortless. Various therapists called and said I should be making greeting cards and calendars. I thought it would be a fabulous way to make a living—if it paid! Well, it does, and it's getting better and better. I get orders every day—and sometimes the callers will break down in tears in reaction to my drawings.

I've also received a lot of letters. One woman gave her mother one of my prints, and the mother hung it up on her fridge. She was an alcoholic, but she stopped drinking, and for the first time in her life she and her daughter talked intimately—for hours. They both say it was because of the picture!

When I first began doing my pictures, another business venture had fallen apart. I was threatened with lawsuits, and I was worried that I was going to be in debt for the rest of my life. In response to my prayers, I felt myself actually being lifted and transported over an abyss. I experienced that feeling over and over until the situation was totally resolved. I still get a physical sense of hands on my body lifting me up. Some people call that mystical. I think it's available to anyone who seeks it.

My life is now worthwhile—it's fabulous! I've never had such a ball. I actually find myself singing and humming. I don't have any great hopes or fears for my future. I'm just having a great time.

A Simple Prayer

And in that day ye shall ask me nothing. Verily, verily, I say unto you, Whatsoever ye shall ask the Father in my name, he will give it to you.

Hitherto have ye asked nothing in my name: ask, and ye shall receive, that your joy may be full.

John 16:23–24

Ann and Robert Bauwens have been married for 17 years, and they live in Green Cove Springs, Florida. Bob works as a salesman selling supplies to golf courses, and Ann works part-time in an office. Deeply involved in church work and outreach prayer activities, the couple enthusiastically shared their faith with me.

As I talked with them about their problems in becoming parents, both became very emotional at times. They reveled in discussing their children, Katy, 16, and Robert, 8, and when the interview was complete, Bob gave me a wallet-sized color photograph of his family.

Ann and Bob hugged me when I left them and Bob said, "Whenever you're in this area, John, please feel welcome to come stay with us."

ANN: In 1975 I was living in California and my doctor told me I had a precancerous condition on my cervix. Tissue was removed and biopsied to see if there were any cancer cells. There was no cancer, but when I went back a month later for my follow-up checkup, we discovered that my cervix had scarred shut from the biopsy.

In 1978 I was planning to get married, so I went to a fertility clinic at the University of California in San Francisco. They told me my cervix was now completely sealed—it's called cervical stenosis—plus my uterine walls had grown together, which, as I eventually learned, is termed Asherman's Syndrome. They operated with lots of special equipment, including a laser, to try to correct the problems with the adhesions in my cervix.

The result was that although my uterus stayed open, my cervix was smaller than a tear duct, an opening barely large enough for me to menstruate. I was told I'd never have a baby because I had no way to facilitate sperm, no cervical mucus, and with scar tissue in the uterus, the placenta might detach during pregnancy and cause hemorrhaging.

I'd met Bob before all my operations, and he was aware of my condition. When we married in 1978 he knew that I could never have children. Although I was very upset by this, I accepted the medical prognosis.

• • •

Seven months after the operation, Bob and I were visiting my brother Tom in Jacksonville, Florida. He's a year younger than me and we've always been very close. Tom's an artist, a very kind and thoughtful person. A religious conversion led him to do a lot of Bible study. When he heard my medical story, he asked very quietly, "Would you and Bob like to have a baby?"

"Of course," I replied. "We'd love to have a baby!"

"Can I pray for you?" Tom asked.

Although Bob and I were not very religious, we agreed. Tom opened his Bible and turned to John 16:23 and 24 and read, "Verily, verily I say unto you. Whatsoever ye shall ask the Father in my name, he will give it to you. Hitherto have ye asked nothing in my name: ask, and ye shall receive, that your joy may be full." Then Tom and his wife laid their hands on me and prayed, "You know, Lord, we ask according to your word that you give Annie and Bob a baby."

As Tom prayed, I stood there thinking how wonderful it would be to have a baby. I never thought you could ask the Father for anything. Tom's prayer was very simple and sincere, and I thanked him for it. The whole thing took me by surprise.

BOB: I was also surprised at how eager Tom was to pray for us. It was a very loving prayer, short and without a lot of emotion, but he put himself in a vulnerable position knowing how foolish he'd look if his prayer wasn't answered. But that turned out not to be a problem. Three or four weeks passed, and Ann missed her period. We were pregnant! I say "we" because I knew there was a real relationship between Ann, me, the baby and the Lord. Without Him this would not have been possible. I realized then that God was a reality and my life had changed. It was a mixed blessing, though, because doctors had told us that even if Ann could become pregnant, she might not be able to carry the baby.

We eased our fears with the belief that the Father who gave us this baby would not take it from us. We realized we had to trust God because we had no other choice.

ANN: I told everybody, "My brother prayed for me and

the Lord gave me a baby!" I was so excited that I didn't hold anything back.

I never had a single problem during my pregnancy except at the end when my water broke very suddenly and I was rushed to the hospital. I always had a different doctor at the hospital I went to. The one who examined me that day said, somewhat irritated, "Didn't anybody tell you how dangerous it is for you to carry a baby? You have Asherman's Syndrome."

All I knew was that Tom had prayed for me, I was having a baby, and I was very happy. I would have to have a Caesarean.

Before the operation they warned me that the placenta might not pull away during delivery and if that was the case, I'd have to have a hysterectomy. That was an unsettling prospect, but fortunately, the Caesarean went well.

Bob and I had a six-pound, seven-ounce baby girl, and we named her Kathryn. I remember crying when I heard my daughter cry.

BOB: After the C-section I went with the nurse to wash Katy clean. I gave my daughter her first bath. I remember crying and holding her and thanking God for His wonderful gift. I also asked the Lord to teach me how to love my little girl. I didn't have a clue how to be a good father, but I knew I'd be able to love her through God.

• • •

ANN: After Kathryn was born, we started going to church. We got involved in a prayer group, and our relationship with the Lord solidified. He had not only brought us life, a baby, but He had given us the promise of a new life. I finally understood that Jesus was the answer. I had learned that in catechism as a child, but until we became actively involved in prayer, I didn't know it in my heart. Somehow, He was always standing over there, about six feet away, and I didn't know how to get connected with Him. But then I prayed that He would be in my life, and it happened.

On June 1, 1980, a friend in a Christian band invited us to an evangelical church meeting. After the band played, a man was giving his testimony. Another friend came up to us and said, "You should see what's happening down front. This man is speaking in another language and people are falling over." I'm a real skeptic, so I went to a side aisle to watch.

I couldn't understand a word the man was saying. People were falling down but they seemed very joyful, so Bob and I got in line to see what this was all about. When it was my turn, the man asked me what I wanted. Without thinking, I just blurted out, "I want Jesus in my life"—and down I went.

I remember looking up at Bob and his wide-open mouth. When the man saw him, he said, "Welcome home." And Bob just cried and cried.

That was the beginning of eight years of prayer and learning about God's will.

• • •

We wanted another baby. I prayed John 16:23 and 24 again and again and fully expected to have another baby. It had worked before. But nothing happened this time. I read in Hebrews 11 where Sara had a baby because of her faith. In Psalms it talks about barren women. But nothing I did—no amount of reading, screaming, crying, or praying—helped. I suffered twelve times a year. Our expectations were high, we hoped for the best, we waited . . . and still, nothing happened.

So, in January 1987 I went to a doctor in Jacksonville who attempted a cervical dilation. After several attempts to insert a tiny probe into my cervix, he gave up. He told me that due to the condition of my cervix, it would be very difficult for me to conceive.

I changed my prayers. I said, "Lord, if it's not Your will for me to have a baby, take away my desire." But my desire only increased. The Lord made me realize that everything is His gift, so I gradually let it go. I knew I had to leave myself in His hands and not struggle so much.

In February, our friend Frances McNutt was having dinner with us. We were just having a normal conversation, with no religious stuff or any prayer. We mentioned that we had been praying for eight years for another child. Frances said, "Would you like me to pray for you to have a baby?"

We had nothing to lose.

She prayed very simply. "Lord, please give them a baby."

Two months later a sonogram indicated that I was pregnant! My date of conception was the day after we prayed at dinner with Frances! Seven months after the sonogram and a very healthy pregnancy, our son Robert was born.

BOB: It was a fantastic experience. It was like God said, "See, I told you. I wasn't going to let you down."

You have to trust God because He puts you in a position where you have nothing else to do but to trust Him. That's the position Ann and I were in all that time.

ANN: During those eight years I'd go to the Bible and pick out Scripture and ask the Lord to increase my faith.

I did a lot of cleansing asking the Lord for help. I can't remember all the things I did to get God to help me, but there wasn't anything I could do to hurry His time, His grace, His plan.

I think part of God's plan is that He wants to know that we're looking to Him. When you have children, you talk with them. God wants to do this with His children, He wants to hear from us. So my prayers at that time were ones in which I submitted myself to the Lord in my thoughts and petitions and asked Him to be present in my life.

One thing I'm grateful for during those hard times is that the Lord used us to help other people. We had been through so much that we found it a real blessing to share our faith and prayers with other infertile couples. Through this outreach of loving and praying that the Lord would bless other people, we found that it brought us closer to God.

It's not intimidating to me that Tom and Frances's prayers brought about our miracles. The Lord loves us through other people: If anything, this realization increased my faith. It moves me to pray for other people to bless them the way I was blessed.

If I had a friend who wanted a baby, I'd tell her to have faith and not to worry about being perfect. I'd pray for her like this: "Praise you, Lord, and thank you for all that you have done in my life, for the children that you have blessed me with. Lord, this friend and sister comes to you and asks that your mighty unfailing love and mercy touch her in a very powerful way. That you would show her your great love and that you would give her the desires of her heart. Lord, I pray that you will bring forth a child for this couple, that you will bless this couple with the greatest gift that anyone can receive (other than your son, Jesus Christ), the gift of life. I thank you, Father, and accept your will. We trust and praise you in Jesus' name. Amen."

The Delicate Orchid

It is our ignorance of God, the divine Principle, which produces apparent discord, and the right understanding of Him restores harmony.

Mary Baker Eddy

Jane Hingert-Eiduson was born in 1949 in the Netherlands to parents of German, Dutch, Danish, Chinese, and Indonesian heritage. Her father, a Dutch soldier during World War II, was a prisoner of the Japanese in Indonesia. Her mother was held in a Japanese labor camp during that time.

When she was 16, Jane's family immigrated to Los Angeles where she eventually graduated from a California state college.

I interviewed Jane in her Los Angeles area home shortly after she returned from a Hawaiian honeymoon with her husband, Mark. She teaches at an alternative school for inner-city children where Mark is an administrator. Jane, a slender, dark-eyed, gracious woman, radiated joy and enthusiasm as she talked.

When I was conceived, my parents had suffered from beriberi and malaria, and Mom had typhoid from being in prison camps for four years during World War II. As a result, I was born skinny and allergic to my mom's milk. I was rather fragile as a little girl and was often sick.

As a child, my friends called me "the delicate orchid," because I was so frail. Early on, I convinced myself that it was going to be difficult to survive the pressures of living. I carried this fear with me most of my life.

• • •

Though I did survive my childhood, two abusive marriages assured me that my fears were still grounded, even as an adult. Then, during 1975 while I was working as a teacher in Los Angeles, I came down with symptoms of stiffness, fevers, and skin lesions. I was diagnosed with systemic lupus erythematosus. I was devastated! Everything about my life was challenging. I learned that with the use of steroids, 80% of those with lupus could survive. But I got progressively worse; my condition turned into a central nervous system disease and I'd have paralysis attacks during which part of my face would droop and I'd lose control of my tongue. I also couldn't remember things or spell words during these episodes.

Eventually I lost my teaching job and my credentials, I went on permanent disability, and I was divorced from my second husband. My fear of life seemed to have been well placed.

From 1977 to 1986 my life was just terrible primarily due to my health. A very loyal girlfriend, Julia Roth, would often take me out—but then she wouldn't be able to get me back into my apartment because I had such frequent attacks. I'd become completely paralyzed and she'd have to ask paramedics, taxi drivers, truck drivers, anybody, to help her bring me up the stairs.

In 1978 I begged my doctor to do something to help me. I couldn't live like that anymore. So he increased my dosages of steroids until eventually, the medication lodged in my eyes, I developed cataracts, and I became legally blind. I was getting sicker and sicker. I became so hypoglycemic I had to eat every twenty minutes, because the drop in my blood sugar made me limp.

In 1980, when I was 31, I had a bad paralysis attack, which kept me in bed for a week, in need of 24-hour care. I'd been hospitalized so often the doctors wanted to put me in a permanent nursing home, but fortunately my friends and family protested.

They got a huge calendar and made a schedule so somebody was with me every day and night. There were about thirty house keys floating around, since I couldn't get up to open the door. My friends fed me, bathed me, and took care of my house until I was well enough to get out of bed.

I often thought, "I shouldn't be alive. I'm a liability, drawing money from the government, relying on my friends. But how long will they put up with this?" I was afraid everybody would leave me.

"No, no," they'd say. "You're giving us an opportunity to love and care in a way we never thought we could."

Without my friends, I would have been in a sanitarium, forgotten, and probably dead.

One day in 1982 Julia called me and said, "I met a group of very nice people called Christian Scientists. They study the Bible along with a book called *Science and Health* written by Mary Baker Eddy. The book is about God, prayer, and healing."

She bought me the book and I started reading it, but I

had a hard time because of my poor vision. When my sight was gone, Julia often read the *Christian Science Monitor* to me. The newspaper had a daily religious article. The columns were about God's love for everyone and they often mentioned healings resulting from prayer. Not being a Christian Scientist, I didn't think it applied to me. My condition continued to deteriorate.

• • •

I had one successful cataract operation so the doctor wanted to operate on the second eye. But I'd had a paralysis attack in the hospital so I didn't want anything else to do with doctors and hospitals.

"No, leave the other one alone." I was speaking with a slur, haltingly. I refused any more medical treatments. I'd had enough of hospitals, medicine, and doctors. One of the doctors warned me, "If you go home and don't get treated, you could die."

"I'll sign a release. I'll die. I'm ready," I told him.

"Jane," he said, "there is nothing more we can do for your lupus. Ask your friends to pray for you."

This really struck me. I thought, "My doctor is telling me to pray?"

I had no other choice—I asked Julia to help me find those Christian Scientists. She found out they had reading rooms for people to study Christian Science, so I had a friend drive me to the nearest one.

I wobbled into the reading room carrying a parasol to keep the sun off my skin. I told the librarian about my lupus and how sick I was. I explained that I wanted to know more about how her church healed people by praying. She gave me a copy of the *Christian Science Journal*, a magazine about their religion, and told me about their church services, testimony meetings, literature, and lectures.

I asked what the cost was for all of this.

"Nothing."

I figured I had nothing to lose. I tried to talk more about my lupus, but she cut me off and said, "Honey, it will all go away."

So that week, I went to a Christian Science church service and I talked to the woman from the reading room afterwards. She gave me a copy of *Science and Health*, but I just put it aside when I got home.

Later on, I had to call the woman to tell her I was too sick to come back to their church. She suggested I call a Christian Science practitioner. "They're experienced Christian Scientists who help people through prayer."

At this point, I'd sought help everywhere. During the twelve-year course of my illness, I had tried Science of Mind, diets, exercise, and Buddhists chanted for me. A doctor claimed he'd cure me if I paid him seven thousand dollars. A group spoke in tongues and laid hands on me, trying to help, but I had an attack and was rushed to an emergency room. But by then, even the doctors had given up on traditional treatments and told me to pray. So I picked a practitioner in the *Journal* and called her.

I tried to tell the practitioner that I was disabled but she wouldn't hear of it. She said, "No, you're not disabled." I thought it was sort of strange that she wouldn't even listen to me talk about my condition. She asked me to read Psalms 119 in the Bible and pages 390 to 396 in *Science and Health* and said that she'd pray for me.

So I read the passages a few times. The first one in *Science and Health* said, "It is our ignorance of God, the divine Principle, which produces apparent discord, and the right understanding of Him restores harmony." I also read the 23rd Psalm. Soon after I finished reading, I experienced a warm energy spreading up from my toes through my whole body. It was an incredible sensation while it lasted, then after the feeling passed, I felt completely cleansed.

I really felt an instant transformation. Although I hadn't driven in months, I suddenly had a strong urge to go to the beach. I put a big note on the dashboard saying, "If I'm found unconscious, this is my medical number, doctor, and friends to call," and I drove myself to the beach.

Later, I telephoned the practitioner to tell her that I felt better and I'd even gone for a drive.

She wasn't even surprised. She just gave me more citations to read.

By the third day I was seeing out of the eye that hadn't been operated on, and I could easily read the citations I'd been given. I called the practitioner and told her I'd experienced a miracle. I could see out of both eyes, even without my contact lenses.

She said, "There are no miracles."

She explained that a miracle would mean only select people could receive the grace of God and be healed, whereas God's benefits and love are for everybody.

On the fourth day, I went to see my doctor for my three-month checkup. He was shocked: All of my tests for the presence of lupus were negative!

I was also more than a little bit shocked. My turnaround was so sudden.

When I asked the practitioner how she'd healed me in four days after I had suffered so terribly for twelve years, she said she didn't do it, it was God. In her prayers she perceived me as a perfect being unscathed by illness or weakness. She did what Jesus did by never accepting physical appearances. That's why she refused to hear me when I said I was disabled. She saw in me the perfect child of God, harmonious, healthy, the way I was meant to be, the way we are all born to be.

I had always accepted the lupus and the cataracts, as if a court had sentenced me. I accepted my limitations. I was afraid of the disease and I believed I was sick because the doctors and the tests told me it was true.

My practitioner explained, "You are only now beginning to see your true inheritance as a child of God."

• • •

My healing came quickly, probably because I was so humbled by my physical disabilities. But when I was healed, it was more than a rebirth, it was like a birth. Physically I improved very quickly, but it took longer to gain the emotional and spiritual understanding of the healing.

In answer to my fears that the lupus would return, the practitioner explained, "Once you're healed of something, there are no retrograde steps," and she gave me more passages from the Bible and *Science and Health* to study. In order to understand what had happened to me, I became a student of Christian Science. I learned that God is limitless. I think I'm just starting to get a sense of what He or She really is.

I've learned that prayer is more about gratitude than asking for things; it's an awakening of my spiritual relationship to God, a relationship that's there for me and for everybody.

When I pray, it's informal, an aligning of my thought

with the way God meant life to be for me, harmonious and joyful. I pray daily to know that there's a loving God controlling everything including me. From that knowledge, I think all healing flows.

• • •

A year after my healing, I went to see my doctor about returning to work. He couldn't believe I was in such good health.

I told him I'd been studying *Science and Health*. I was very sheepish. "A practitioner has been helping me pray and I've been playing tennis. Do you think I could go back to work?"

He encouraged me to keep on doing what I was doing. It was time for me to join the working world again.

In order to work again, I had to attend a seminar to reactivate my teaching credentials. My old insecurities returned and I was fearful I wouldn't do well. When I looked at the final test paper, it was a blur! I panicked. I thought I was going blind again—that I wasn't really healed!

All the lupus symptoms—fever, sweating and weakness—returned. So I left the seminar and went to a friend's house. I told her I was losing my eyesight again. "I had a good year and now it's over."

She looked at the test paper I'd brought and started laughing. "I can't read it either!" she said. The teacher had copied the test so often it *was* a blur. The moment I realized my vision hadn't failed me, all of my other symptoms disappeared. Though it was a frightening hour, it was a good lesson about my susceptibility to fear. I was like Job in the Bible when he said, "The very thing I fear has come upon me."

Practicing Christian Science means replacing the fear

and limitation I'd accepted for myself since birth with my true identity as God's creation. Now I see myself as being on a wonderful spiritual journey, taking baby steps but shedding fears every step of the way. My transformation is still a daily process, but having experienced that powerful healing of lupus is a constant reminder of my potential, and of the power of prayer.

Racing for the Lord

For I the Lord thy God will hold thy right hand, saying unto thee, Fear not; I will help thee.

Isaiah 41:13

Lake Speed is a professional race car driver on the National Association for Stock Car Auto Racing (NASCAR) circuit, the biggest in the U.S. At speeds up to 200 mph, he races 32 times a year at racetracks from California to Florida. His race cars cost $50,000 to $60,000 each, and major sponsors typically spend $2 million to $5 million to make a team competitive.

Lake ("Yes, Lake Speed is my real name") and his wife Ricẽ have three children, ages 7, 5, and 3. He also has a 23-year-old son from his first marriage. I interviewed Lake, a short, sturdy man, in his office near his spacious, rural home in Kannapolis, North Carolina. He wore a pullover, khaki pants, and loafers.

Lake began his racing career competing in go-karts, small open-wheeled vehicles that resemble bumper cars and reach speeds of 150 mph. He was a six-time national go-kart champion.

I've made numerous auto-racing films and have always enjoyed the "down home," unpretentious attitude of stock car drivers, and Lake is no exception. He told me about competing at Alabama's Talladega Speedway in May 1983. While leading the race, he heard a voice speaking to him.

There were ten or twelve laps left in the race and I was on the backstretch when a small voice spoke to me, a voice I'd never heard before.

The voice said, "Lake, what are you going to do if you win here, too?"

Stock car racing is as tough a competition as you'll find anywhere on God's green earth. In the beginning of my career, I had serious doubts about competing because I had no contacts or financial support and I wasn't part of the racing clique. But here I was, leading a very big race, only three years after starting out—from scratch—on the NASCAR circuit.

When I heard that voice it really shook me up, because it was similar to an experience I'd had in 1978 at the Le Mans racetrack in France, when I won the World's Championship of Karting. I'd spent nineteen years in go-kart racing and when I won the World's Championship, the only non-European to ever take that title, I had to stop and think about my next goal.

I remember standing on the winner's podium engulfed by the noise of the celebration, and suddenly realizing there was only one person I really knew at the race. I wondered what this was all for: I was so obsessed with winning, I'd lost sight of everything else. I was so self-centered that my wife had divorced me and taken our son.

I had lots of trophies but few friends and not much joy in my life.

My thought at Le Mans, of "What is this all for?" vividly came back to me when I heard that questioning voice at Talladega. Although I'd progressed in my racing career, my personal life was pretty empty, and that hadn't really changed since Le Mans. What was I doing with my life?

Near the end of the Talladega race I had a bad pit stop and eventually finished third. Afterwards I returned to an apartment that wasn't a real home, to a live-in girlfriend, but not a family. Racing was fun, but it wouldn't last forever. And I wondered if people really loved me, or were they just enamored with what I did?

I wondered, where was the truth in the world that you could really sink your teeth into?

The little voice came to me again and told me, "If you want to know the truth, try reading the Bible."

• • •

At the age of fifteen, I'd been baptized and joined a church. I figured I was saved, I had my ticket to heaven and could go on my merry way. I knew my Bible verses and went to church every Sunday and did whatever I wanted the rest of the week. I even took three semesters of Bible in the Christian college I attended. But I never put the whole picture together.

After the race, my girlfriend Ricẽ and I sat on the edge of the bed and started reading the Bible. Our relationship was as worldly and as crazy as it could be. I was racing all over the country, and if she didn't come with me, I had other girlfriends. She had her friends when I wasn't around, too. Both of us played the same game and neither one of us was getting anywhere.

Once we started reading the Bible, it didn't take us long to realize that God really loved us. But He also had ways for us to live our lives. There were things we shouldn't do. Many of these were things we did on a regular basis; things that smelled good, tasted good, and felt good.

We continued to read and go to church on a regular basis when I wasn't racing. Ricẽ was a research nurse at the time, and some of the women at her clinic invited us to attend their church. We went to the church, which was on the other side of the tracks, in a pretty rough neighborhood.

It was very different from any experience I had ever had in church. I was used to things being really solemn and reverent. But these folks were having a great time. It was like a party. They were all singing and happy. Yet, they were very serious. It was the first time I'd been in a church service where people really worshipped the Lord. I began to recognize the spirit that I'd been reading about in the New Testament.

The pastor made an altar call and asked, "Is there anyone here who wants to turn their life over to the Lord Jesus Christ?" I heard that little voice again saying, "Lake, you wanted to know the truth, what life was all about. You've been running your own life since you were 23 years old and you made a mess out of it, chasing material things that were here today and gone tomorrow. Why don't you turn your life over to me and let me guide you?"

Tears came down my face and I made my decision right there. I said, "I'm tired of trying to figure out how to be happy and successful. I can't do it. I'm ready to let you try."

As I left that pew to make a confession of my faith I heard another voice screaming at me, "If you go down front you will never race again!"

At that moment, I didn't care if I ever raced again. I was going to give the Lord a try.

As it turned out, I could do both. Because I was willing to put my faith in the Lord and I was willing to give up racing, God gave it back to me. He said that in the past, I'd always raced for Lake Speed; now I'd be racing for Him. He gave me my unique talent so I could witness and testify for the Lord in public as a race car driver. I could do much more for the Lord this way than I could in any other capacity.

My real prayer life began when I went down front and prayed and asked the Lord Jesus Christ to come into my life. From that day forward I knew that I could speak to Him and hear Him.

• • •

My next significant prayer experience occurred in 1985 when a first-class NASCAR racing team asked me to be their new driver. The only problem was they didn't have a sponsor.

Ricẽ and I had gotten married in 1984. She had had the same experience that I had in that little church. And so we both prayed to know whether we should leave Jackson, Mississippi, where we had our roots and families, and move to Charlotte, North Carolina, to join the team. I never, ever thought I would leave Jackson. My family had been there forever—my Dad had been mayor there—it was home.

But we felt the Lord was leading us. It would give me a greater opportunity to continue the talks and testimony

I'd been giving about how my life had changed through Christ. It would also be a giant leap of faith to join a new team without a sponsor in a new town.

We prayed and prayed and then we packed up and moved. We trusted God that we had made the right decision.

As the team prepared for the racing season, Ricẽ and I prayed every day for a sponsor. During that time I often read from Isaiah 41:13: "For I the Lord will hold thy right hand, saying unto thee, Fear not; I will help thee."

For several months I helped the team owners, calling people, holding meetings, and doing everything I could to raise money. It was discouraging, but every now and then I'd hear that voice say, "Lake, why don't you trust me?"

The Daytona 500 is the Super Bowl of stock car racing in terms of its importance, but it's the first race of the season. As the race approached, the team was running out of money and still no sponsor had appeared. We decided to race anyway. If the team had to shut down after Daytona, so be it.

Sometimes teams arrange for partial sponsorship at races. Usually they are associate sponsors who get their name on a small part of the race car for just the one race. We practiced and then qualified for the race with our car, a plain white Pontiac with a big blue number and no sponsor's name.

The day before the big race I was watching a preliminary event from the Goodyear Tires hospitality suite in the stands. Ray Brown, a man I had briefly met in the garage area, sat down next to me. He'd never been to a stock car race before, so he asked me to explain what was going on.

The race started and all the cars were running door handle to door handle. The pit stops were quick. A car spun out, and this guy was getting real excited. He wouldn't leave my side.

When the race was over he said, "This is the most exciting thing I've ever seen. I'm with Nationwide Auto Parts. I came here to work out a sponsorship with a team, but I've never been able to connect with them. Would y'all be interested in an associate sponsor?"

So the next day I started the Daytona 500 with the painted-on sponsor's name still wet on the car. The team owners told Ray Brown they were so grateful for his signing on as an associate sponsor for the year that they put his company's name on the car just as if he were a full sponsor.

The appeal of racing for me is competition. I enjoy trying to beat other teams, getting my car to run a little better, a little faster. To outrun competitors who have more funding.

I eventually finished second, after about four hours of racing, to Bill Elliott. A tough competitor, Bill had major sponsorship and won a lot of big races later that year.

After crossing the finish line I was driving into the garage area, and the first guy I saw was Ray Brown. He was completely unglued. "This is great! Wonderful! We're not going to take our company name off your car. Don't worry about sponsorship. I'll get the money somehow. We'll sponsor you fully for the rest of the year." I was elated. As I got out of my car, I realized the TV cameras were turned toward me instead of staying with the winner in the victory lane. A guy stuck a microphone in front of me and said, "You came to Daytona with no sponsor and you finished second. What does this mean to you?"

There were a lot of people around me hugging and celebrating and at that very noisy instant I heard this little familiar voice say, "I told you so, Lake. I told you that I'd do it."

I just burst into tears and started bawling like a baby. I don't remember what I told the camera but I thanked the Lord for giving me a good run and answering my prayers.

The next day I flew to New York to be on morning TV and we got a lot of publicity. Most people thought I was emotional because I finished second. But placing in the race didn't have anything to do with my emotions. It was the answered prayer that moved me.

Prayer is going before the Lord and just communicating with Him. I talk to the Lord in my consciousness, or verbally; sometimes I sing, sometimes I holler. I think God cries over those who don't pray. I really think God wants a relationship with people. If you care deeply about your wife or your children and all of a sudden they don't communicate with you, it hurts. I think God is deeply hurt when we as His children turn our backs on Him.

I really want to show people that you can be a Christian and be a winner. You don't have to drive around in an old beat-up car with flapping fenders. You can be a victorious Christian, live a victorious life.

I'm convinced God chuckles when he looks at me. "Ol' Lake down there was really messed up. Now he's turned around and knows the truth. He's trying hard but he still stumbles. I have to pick him up now and then and dust him off, but he's trying."

Even though I used to party and play and have a big ol' time I have a whole lot more fun now. I'm really enjoying my new life racing for the Lord!

A Tremendous Bullet of Light

Most people consider the course of events as natural and inevitable. They little know what radical changes are possible through prayer.

Paramahansa Yogananda

Bob and Catherine Saltzman were married in 1985 and live in Ridgway, Colorado, with their sons David, 8, and Matt, 13. Bob, a former Green Beret officer and vice president of the largest commercial real estate firm in the United States, is now the executive director of the Institute of Ecolonomics, a non-profit organization founded by actor Dennis Weaver to offer innovative solutions to environmental problems. Catherine is a writer, consultant and former international model and syndicated health and beauty columnist.

Bob was brought up in the Congregational and Methodist Churches and also attended Catholic Church services for a time. Catherine went to Catholic schools and church as a child but in her late teens she became an agnostic. While working in Los Angeles as a model and actress in television commercials, she read a book that changed her life.

CATHERINE: The *Autobiography of a Yogi*, by Paramahansa Yogananda, was given to me by a coworker in 1972. The book had a tremendous effect on my life. Yogananda was a great lover of God and his writing reflected a deep passion for the divine, which touched my heart and brought back childhood memories of reading about the lives of the saints. Yogananda explained the mystical religious experience, something I hadn't thought about for years. As I read, I kept thinking, "Of course, now it all makes sense."

That book propelled me out of my agnosticism. It made me realize that I didn't have to take things on blind faith, I could practice meditation and see for myself.

Yogananda founded Self-Realization Fellowship (SRF) in 1920 to teach scientific techniques of yoga meditation for attaining direct, personal experience of God. When Bob and I were married, we were both active in SRF and meditated and prayed morning and night. Yogananda taught that true prayer works like mathematics, being based on precise laws that govern all creation, and is a daily necessity for harmonious living.

• • •

In 1987, our 18-month-old son, David, fell and hit the back of his head on the cement sidewalk outside our home in Encinitas, California. He cried very hard so I called an osteopath who had worked on David previously, but she was out of the country for a month. David calmed down and seemed fine but, as a precaution, I took him to another osteopath who said that indeed there had been a compression of the bones at the back of his head. She worked on him and recommended we see our own osteopath, who was a child specialist, as soon as possible.

That night David didn't sleep well and in the morning he had a fever. We called our pediatrician, who told us to give him lots of liquids, rest and Tylenol. Because David was still hot that evening, Bob took him out for a walk in his stroller.

BOB: It was just turning dark, and as I pushed the stroller down the street it all of a sudden felt like a brake had been applied to the wheels. I looked down to see David's feet dragging on the sidewalk. Then I saw that his body was stiff as a board and that he was evidently having a seizure. His face was turning blue as I picked him up and ran home. I frantically whispered, "*Dear God, please help me. I don't know what to do.*"

CATHERINE: When I saw David I knew it was serious and called the pediatrician's office. God answered that first desperate prayer because a nurse happened to be working late and picked up the phone. She told us to keep him upright and to make sure he didn't swallow his tongue. David started to breathe and relaxed somewhat and we rushed him to the pediatrician's office. The doctor told us that it was probably a viral infection and not to be alarmed. David was given a shot of Phenobarbital to stop the seizures. Unfortunately, it turned out that he was allergic to the medication. After we took him home he had a fever of 106 degrees and more seizures.

The fever didn't go away and a few days later, at the doctor's office, we were told it might be spinal meningitis. Bob held David while the doctor did a spinal tap, which is very painful. I had to leave the room while that was happening to my precious baby. I didn't want David to see me cry. I decided to call the SRF Retreat in Encinitas, to talk to a nun I knew there.

She advised that I close my eyes, take a few deep breaths and pray. She reminded me that the doctor was a child of God and suggested that we pray that God would work through him and that he would be receptive to God's guidance. "I want you to visualize David right now as healthy," she said softly. "Always see him as perfectly normal no matter what evidence appears to the contrary. Always hold the thought that he is perfect." She said she would also give our names to SRF's Worldwide Prayer Circle. This international prayer circle was started by Yogananda many years ago. SRF monastics and thousands of lay members all over the world pray twice a day for world peace and for those who have requested specific help.

Thankfully, the test for spinal meningitis was negative. We were relieved and took David home. However, several nights later his fever was still alarmingly high, so we went to an emergency room. After the doctors there ran some tests, they sent us to a hospital in nearby San Diego. By this time he had endured fifteen days of high fever. Over the next five days nine specialists examined him. They inserted an IV in his left foot and administered antibiotics. We told them about David falling and hitting his head but they said that wasn't the problem. They were suspecting an auto-immune disease. They were loading him with Tylenol and we started to see signs of liver deterioration. He was so weak he couldn't even lift his head.

BOB: We were praying continually and either Catherine or I were always with David in the hospital. He was rapidly deteriorating and they thought he might have juvenile rheumatoid arthritis because he had broken out in a painful rash, which is one of the symptoms. They also suggested he might have Lupus. The doctors didn't really have a clear diagnosis.

On the fifth day in the hospital the head doctor said he was perplexed and wanted to give David steroids as an experiment. Catherine's response was a firm, "Over my dead body!" I was tempted to just pick David up and run out of the hospital. It was so obvious that nothing was working. Finally we asked to take David out on a pass in order to get other opinions. They reluctantly agreed and we left to visit some holistic practitioners because it appeared that we had reached the end of the line with conventional medicine.

David's spirits really picked up when we brought him home, so I called the doctor at the hospital and said, "David's happy here. Let us keep him at home and we'll let you know what's happening." They agreed because they didn't have a definite diagnosis and an established treatment to pursue. That turned out to be very lucky for us.

CATHERINE: Now we're at home with this really sick child, giving him around-the-clock care and taking him to different alternative practitioners. We'd see signs of improvement but then new problems would arise. By this time the medical doctors had convinced us it wasn't the fall that was the problem. This went on for another ten days and we were getting exhausted. Some of our family lived nearby, and they were doing everything they could to help. But they had their own busy lives and there was only so much they could do. Bob had not been able to return to his real estate job, which meant no income was being generated. Our savings were rapidly disappearing. Then SRF members, many of whom we didn't even know, started showing up at the house to offer their help. Every few days someone would come to clean the house, or do the laundry or bring groceries. For two months there was never a night that someone didn't bring us dinner. There was no formal committee, just people who wanted to help us.

It was during this time that we decided to have a Prayer Circle meeting just for David in our home. We didn't know if anyone had ever done that before. He still had an angry red rash that he constantly scratched, causing scabs to form. These wounds were painful and constantly irritating to him. His left leg, where the IV had been inserted, had sort of shriveled and the foot had turned in at the ankle. There were a lot of educated guesses as to why that had happened but no one knew for certain. The worst part was that our formerly happy son had become very withdrawn and traumatized. We wondered whether he would be able to handle all the new people in the house. On the evening of the Prayer Circle meeting, I took David into his bedroom and, surprisingly, he just quietly nestled up to me as everyone in the room prayed for him.

The prayer session lasted about twenty minutes and followed the outline Yogananda gave, which includes meditation and a special healing technique that involves consciously directing life energy to the person being helped. We began with a prayer by Yogananda that in part goes, "Heavenly Father, Thou are omnipresent; Thou art in all Thy children; manifest Thy healing presence in his body." Every person in the room was intensely and lovingly focused on David. I was very touched by the way everyone concentrated on sending healing thoughts to him.

Bob and I saw results from the prayer session immediately: we were enormously relieved when the awful itching from the rash completely stopped. David never again needed any salve or medication for discomfort, although the rash itself didn't go away for almost a year. Some of the people who prayed with us later called and said, "I went home in a state of peace and happiness. I was inspired for days because of the prayer session. Can we do it again?"

So about a week later we had another session, which again made use of the two fundamental aspects of scientific prayer: thought and energy. During the session you could almost see the loving willpower of the people in the room. It made a deep impression on me. Afterwards, Bob carried David outside and he high-fived the people as they left. Everyone laughed and it was wonderful to see David so lively.

When we came back inside, I sat David in a big chair in the living room and went into the kitchen to make tea. Suddenly I noticed something out of the corner of my eye. I turned and there was David walking towards me. He hadn't taken a step in a month! His twisted left foot was actually flat on the floor. I couldn't believe it. My whole body felt like Jell-O and I had to hang on to the stove. Then the incredulous feeling was replaced by one of peace and gratitude. David smiled.

Thirty-eight days had passed when our osteopath returned from her trip. After examining David, she said, "My goodness, why didn't the hospital do a CAT Scan?" She confirmed that the fall had severely compressed his occipital bones and put pressure on the back of the brain, which, she explained, can cause a high fever and an immune system "shut down." She treated him—an osteopath subtly manipulates and corrects structure—and on day forty, David's temperature returned to normal.

Unfortunately, we still weren't out of the crisis. David had become severely anemic and there was fear that his organs were going to be permanently damaged. The new doctors we were seeing were holistically inclined, but they too thought he had juvenile rheumatoid arthritis, and wanted to do blood transfusions for the anemia. Other practitioners advised not to do the transfusions but to constantly give him fresh, dark green leafy and red vegetable juices, along with specific natural supplements. We were doing this continually, but results were slow. Meanwhile, Bob wasn't working. We were living off our savings and trying to decide if we should risk the transfusions. We were scared.

BOB: I was spending every night in David's room. Catherine and I were both under a lot of pressure and I feared for our health as well. Neither one of us had had much sleep and every day we made decisions that potentially affected whether David lived or died. I slept in David's room and if he'd breathe funny, I'd be up in an instant. His breath was my breath. It's amazing what you hear as a parent.

One dawn I suddenly awoke, and instead of feeling alarm or anxiety, I felt such love and peace, and for a moment, I saw over his crib a full-winged angel. She looked sort of like a Christmas angel and her hands were facing towards the crib and I felt love just pouring out of her. I'd never experienced anything like it. From that moment on, I knew that everything was going to be okay.

We kept praying to God about the blood transfusion. When we thought about doing it, there was a feeling of confusion. It was a subtle feeling that it just didn't fit—it simply didn't feel right. In quiet meditation, it became clear to us that it was not the way to go.

CATHERINE: After the Prayer Circle meeting, David's whole body was tremendously strengthened by the osteopath's work. Little by little his blood became less anemic. After six months we felt we were out of the woods, though he still required extensive care for the next year. We received no traditional medical treatment after we left the hospital except for blood tests and consultations on the blood work. We did receive a great deal of well-meaning advice from friends and acquaintances, and we were often torn about which way to go. So we always prayed that God would work through whoever was treating David. We felt that God led us day by day to the right people.

One of the SRF nuns consoled me during this time and reminded me that David was God's child and that I need not hold on too tight. She said, "God has watched over this child's soul before you were his mother and He will always watch over it. Do your best but leave the results up to God."

With the help of all the people who prayed for us, we came out of this difficult experience with changed hearts. We put our lives and the children's lives in God's hands. We now pray, "Lord, you know what we want. But we don't always know what is best. Bless us that the highest good may happen for all." Then we make every effort to act in the way we feel guided while at the same time trusting God to take care of the outcome.

Sri Daya Mata, the president of SRF, once gave a beautiful description of prayer. She said, "Prayer is not an idle undertaking. When offered with sincerity and faith, prayer is like a tremendous bullet of light, shooting at the darkness of suffering. Prayer has immense power to help others—physically, mentally and spiritually."

BOB: Listening to God's guidance can turn into something big! To me prayer is the compass that guides sincere effort down the path that God has charted for us. David is eight now and goes strong until ten at night. He has so much energy and strength. He's a fabulous skier. That child was so blessed, and has so much spiritual energy stored up, he is set for life!

Emily

> *Yet it pleased the Lord to bruise him; he hath put him to grief: when thou shalt make his soul an offering for sin, he shall see his seed, he shall prolong his days, and the pleasure of the Lord shall prosper in his hand.*
>
> *Isaiah 53:10*

James Imonti is a 49-year-old jewelry designer who lives in Providence, Rhode Island. Married to Lovey, his fourth wife, he has a two-year-old daughter and three other children.

I interviewed James in his small jewelry store at night after it had closed. The chair he sat in was illuminated by a single overhead light. Behind him was a wall covered with a jumble of photos, memos, and material relating to his jewelry designing craft. James, lean and muscular with short, dark hair, reminded me of the actor Jack Palance. He spoke emotionally and with a slightly raspy voice about his problems that began as a youth, growing up with parents who never encouraged him to go to college.

In 1968 James joined the Air Force instead, and there he was introduced to marijuana.

I got busted for smoking marijuana and spent five months in the Air Force brig. I survived by reading the book of

Psalms, my first strong experience with prayer. I'd been baptized in the Catholic Church and I'd always believed in God though I never went to church. After I got out of the brig, I went AWOL so many times the Air Force gave me an undesirable discharge.

Then I started selling marijuana. I made a lot of money, but I wasn't proud about selling drugs. I really wanted to do something with my life but I just never developed any thought-out life plan. Eventually I got busted and was sentenced to one to ten years in Danbury Federal Prison in Rhode Island.

I knew I'd screwed up, but I was too immature to understand my emotions or behavior. So I turned my prison time into a monastic experience. I prayed, read the Bible, took yoga classes, read and wrote poetry. Eventually I was so at peace with myself, it didn't matter to me when I got out.

But after a year and a half in prison I was released in 1971. I fell back into my less than monastic routine, smoking pot and not being terribly productive. Then a year after my release from prison I met a young woman who started talking to me about Christ, the Lord, and being saved. She took me to a coffeehouse where I met a group of people who said they'd pray for me. A guy named Dwight asked me if I would accept Christ. I told him I liked to smoke pot and have sex and I thought this was probably against their beliefs.

"Would you be willing to pray to have these desires removed?" Dwight asked.

It was a profound moment for me. I didn't think accepting Christ had any connection with removing anything but I agreed out of a sincere desire to be Christlike. I prayed with those people that Jesus would be my personal savior and that he'd end my desire for marijuana and sex. And I meant every word of it. After a few hours there was only myself and Barbara, a very attractive woman, left from the group. I already felt transformed, because oddly, I felt no sexual attraction to her. I looked at her like she was my sister.

A few months later I met a former monk who was setting up a Christian household which I decided to join. I started going to a coffeehouse run by a Pentecostal Assembly of God church. For the next year and a half, I became extremely involved in the church. Then in 1973 we traveled around the U.S. and Mexico in a van, staying at missions and giving Christian talks.

While we were in Mexico, I smoked marijuana once in a while just to relax. My real downfall didn't come until San Francisco. I visited a buddy there who was shooting heroin and somehow I ended up getting high with him. I quickly threw away a year and a half of spiritual growth: By the time I got home to Rhode Island I was back on drugs.

If I wasn't using drugs, I was drinking, and vice versa. Occasionally, I'd have sober periods where I'd do yoga and run, then inevitably I'd go back to using drugs. All the while, I managed to hold down a variety of jobs: sign painter, graphic artist, and construction worker.

Drugs provided me with energy and they anesthetized me so I could work twice as hard and feel no pain. I ran the Boston Marathon one year after shooting heroin. It extended my threshold of pain and I actually ran a fast race. But despite what I thought of as the advantages, using drugs interrupted my spiritual life, and I'd always feel guilty.

By 1984 I was so hooked on heroin that I couldn't stop. My wife left me. She and our three kids moved in with her sister and I'd see the children on the weekend. I still loved my kids, drugs or no drugs.

One Saturday afternoon I took my kids, ages six, four, and two, to the park. I'd done a morning shot of heroin because my body had built up such an addiction to it that if I didn't shoot up, I'd get sick. I was using eight to ten bags a day, a lot of dope.

About four P.M. in the park with the kids I started to get sick. I had my youngest daughter, Emily, in a backpack. I told the kids to run on ahead and I'd make some peanut butter sandwiches from stuff I had in the backpack. When I put the backpack down, Emily ran off to be with her sister and brother.

This gave me time to inject myself, which I did in a few minutes. But when I finished, I looked up and didn't see my two-year-old.

"Where's Emily?" I yelled to Julie and James. "Where'd she go?"

I was rushing around shouting for Emily when a man found her in the park pond. Emily had fallen in the water, and it looked like she'd drowned. The guy gave her CPR and I explained to everyone who had gathered that I'd been making sandwiches and didn't know what had happened. Inside, I felt so ashamed. I was numb with guilt that I'd let something happen to Emily. I was suicidal I was in so much pain. And the only way I could survive was to shoot more heroin.

For the two and a half years Emily lay in a coma in

intensive care, I was continuously shooting heroin. I virtually lived in the hospital with Emily. I stole syringes and money from the nurses to get heroin. When I wasn't in the hospital, I lived on the street or in abandoned houses.

I loathed myself. The only way I could survive was to completely escape from reality by numbing my senses with drugs and alcohol. Then I hit rock bottom one night, down by a river in Providence. It was a bad area, dirty, and full of addicts. My veins were starting to collapse, and it was becoming harder and harder to inject myself. I was also becoming psychotic. I fell down and dropped my syringe and heroin. I slid down the muddy riverbank and just lay there in the darkness.

In the midst of all this sickness and distress, I felt a quietness and a Christlike sense of grace. It didn't matter where I was physically; what mattered was where I was going spiritually.

For almost three years, starting with the day of Emily's accident, I'd lived a nightmare: I'd overdosed seven times; went in and out of detox centers; broke my leg jumping off a building; robbed people; and I'd almost died from using an infected needle. I'd even received the last rites from a priest.

Lying at the bottom of the muddy riverbank, I realized that if I hadn't died from all this, there must be a reason to live. So on that night, I turned myself in to the police. I had charges against me for credit card fraud, theft, possession of heroin and cocaine, shoplifting, and receiving stolen goods. I went to detox for a while, then the court brought me back and I was given the chance to go to a Salvation Army rehab program.

Before I could do that, though, I had an outstanding

felony warrant against me in another town. The federal marshals picked me up. But instead of taking me to face the warrant and probably serve more prison time, they mistakenly delivered me to the Salvation Army center. That was my first good break.

When I arrived at the Salvation Army Center my life turned around. For eight days I was so sick I could hardly move. I wanted to shoot up the whole time, but nothing I could do would bring that about. Every time I'd try to get high, something, somehow would prevent it. It's as if God knew what was going on and said, "I've got to help this poor bastard." Sensing this intervention, I began to pray, meditate, and read the Bible every day.

Several months into my recovery, Emily died. Though I'd prepared myself for her death for the three years she was in a coma, it was still a tremendous blow. I finally started to get honest with myself and I took advantage of all the tools available to me in the rehab program. I told my wife and family what had actually caused Emily's death—my own addiction. All I wanted was to be honest. Nothing mattered except making peace with myself and with God. Drugs take you down and ruin your life. Drugs are less powerful than prayer because drugs can't make you love more or bring you closer to God.

I started to change, and everyone could see it. I was praying, fasting, exercising, reading Scripture, helping people, and I was doing so well that the Salvation Army put me on their payroll while I was in their rehab program.

My prayer every morning was, "God, please keep me clean and sober. Please restore me to sanity. I turn my life over to Your care through Your son, Jesus Christ, my Lord. I am willing that you should remove every defect of character which stands in the way of my usefulness to you and my companions. Help me to do your bidding and to help any sick or suffering addict or alcoholic."

• • •

Last week I spoke at a detox meeting and ran into an addict I know. I said, "Man, don't be ashamed about your addiction with me. It took me years to kick it. My first treatment was in 1970 in a federal pen. Don't be embarrassed. I will pray for you. What else can I do but pray?"

My spiritual life today consists of prayer, meditation, and helping other people. It's guided by love and honesty. I keep what I have by giving it away. If you give out love, honesty, and spirituality, that's what you get back. "As ye soweth, so shall ye reap." That's my philosophy. And I pray every day. I love to pray. I try to live my life as a prayer. My prayer is natural and spontaneous and I become like a child. I really love that about me, and I think that God loves that about me, too.

Sometimes I'll take some nugget of wisdom from the Bible, meditate on it and then sit quietly. Sometimes I'll chant or sing. I'm not afraid to ask God for things. But I don't think it really matters how you dialogue with God. He's going to give me what I need instead of what I want—but when I pray at least He knows I'm trying!

Some of my prayers are very emotional. Sometimes I'll pull my car over and cry because I have so much grief. Sometimes I pray to my Emily. If I get into a jam I'll say, "Oh, I know somebody who can put me in touch with this spiritual giant up there!" I ask Emily to pray to Jesus for me because I think she's got some clout up there. I'm a long-distance runner and I've seen my daughter, Emily, with me while I'm running. I know that she is with me.

Emily's death was the most horrible tragedy imaginable. I grieve for her every day and my sadness and remorse are unthinkable. As preposterous as it may sound, though, for me it was almost like Christ dying. Emily's death ultimately caused my resurrection.

I will grieve for Emily always. The kids and I visit Emily's grave all the time. I talk to her, and I usually cry, but we always end up laughing and remembering things she used to do. Though I couldn't talk about Emily's death at first, now talking about her keeps her alive for me. Sometimes I'll hear a song and I'll tell whomever I'm with, "That's an Emily song."

• • •

When I first started dating my present wife Lovey, I reached a point where I had to tell her about my life and about Emily. When I finished confessing, she very quietly said, "Thank you." It was like the first time I told the story at a detox meeting. Everyone clapped and hugged me. I thought, "Ye shall know the truth and the truth shall set you free."

The acts of intercession and predestination in my life have no logical explanation other than there is a God, and it's proof that God loves me. I really believe that with all my heart.

A Blessing Is a Prayer

Be merciful unto me, O God, be merciful unto me: for my soul trusteth in thee: yea, in the shadow of thy wings will I make my refuge, until these calamities be overpast.

Psalms 57:1

Sherry Hall is a 52-year-old mother of two daughters, Allison, 7, and Ashley, 9. Her husband, Larry, is an insurance company manager. Sherry worked as an office manager for Goodwill Industries before she became pregnant with their first child. They live in Pacific Palisades, an affluent beach community near Los Angeles.

In order to be uninterrupted during the interview I met Sherry at an empty mobile home that she and her husband own and rent out. Her hair was short, she appeared to wear no makeup, and she was dressed in a running suit. I could smell the nearby ocean as we sat on the floor and talked. As the sun began to set and it grew darker, I felt isolated from the world in that mobile home, and all my attention and thoughts were on Sherry's life-changing prayer experiences.

Sherry often paused before she carefully answered my questions about how prayer had healed her of cancer and infertility.

When I married my second husband Larry in 1971, I told him I wasn't interested in joining the Church of the Latter-Day Saints (the Mormon church), the church he'd been brought up in. That was okay with him because he'd left that church before I met him. I was raised in the Lutheran Church, but hadn't been to any church in a long time.

After Larry and I had been married for about eight or nine years, we both felt a need for spirituality in our lives, so we started searching for a church to join. We visited a Lutheran church, a Mormon church, and several others. I told Larry flat out that there was no way I would ever become a Mormon. Larry's father was always talking about trying to convert me, and I rebelled against that sort of pressure.

One evening we got a phone call from some Mormon missionaries who wanted to come to our house. Larry initially told them we weren't interested in talking with them, but they persuaded him to let them visit.

They actually made several visits and we talked about the Bible and the Book of Mormon and it was all very nice. Finally, I went to the Latter-Day Saints chapel in Pacific Palisades, where I watched a video on Joseph Smith and how he founded the church. It seemed very logical to me: It felt right. I can't really explain why or what happened. I just knew I was home. I experienced a complete turnaround and pretty soon, there was no doubt in my mind that I wanted to be a Mormon. In 1980 I was baptized in the church.

• • •

On a Friday afternoon in 1981 I went to my doctor for my regular checkup. When he touched my throat to check for thyroid problems, he felt a small lump. He asked me if I'd been having any problems with my throat, and I told him I could feel something there when I swallowed.

He asked me to swallow a number of times; then he said, very seriously, "Sherry, you need to go to the hospital for some tests. There is a growth there and I want to have it looked at."

At the hospital I was put under a big machine and scanned for a long time. Afterwards, the doctor had a funny look on his face and he said they wanted to run the test again. He was suddenly very serious.

Later that day, my doctor called me at my office. It was bad news: "The tests indicate cancer. We need to go in and take this out right away."

I was so shocked I needed time to absorb everything. I asked if I could have a couple of days to think. This was all so out of the blue: I wasn't expecting it. He agreed but said I'd have to come in first thing Monday morning so we could set everything up with the hospital. Still in complete shock, I went home and told my husband.

After a miserable Saturday, I went to church on Sunday and told the elders that I needed a blessing. In our church, a blessing is a prayer. The Mormon church doesn't have ordained ministers like other churches, so two lay priesthood holders, called Bishops, would anoint my head with consecrated oil and say the blessing over me.

I sat in a small room in the church, alone with the two elders. I told the Bishop about my tumor. He'd baptized me, so I felt very comfortable with him. The Bishop told me that when he gave a blessing, he prayed within himself so he would say what the Lord wanted him to say. Together, they prayed that I would have strength and courage during this trial. They told me that this experience would draw Larry and me closer together. Throughout the blessing, the Bishop would say a few words, then pause, and then he would start talking. It was as if he was having a conversation with someone else I couldn't hear.

The entire blessing took about ten minutes. At the end, I felt very warm and spiritual and I was close to tears. It was the first church blessing I had ever had, and I really believed that the Lord was talking through these two men. I was somewhat comforted when the Bishop told me I was going to be okay, but naturally I still had doubt. I was new to the church, and cancer invoked a tremendous fear in me.

When I went home I prayed for God to be with me. I was afraid of surgery and I was afraid of cancer. I don't remember specifically praying that it would go away. I didn't read from any Scriptures. I was just talking to God, begging for Him to be with me, and telling Him that I needed strength to get through the operation.

On Monday morning, Larry and I went to the doctor's office. He told me he'd scheduled my operation for the next day. Then he put his hand to my throat and asked me to swallow a number of times. He left the office and returned with another doctor who did the same thing while I just kept swallowing. My doctor left the room to get the X ray. When he came back, they both touched my throat and again asked me to swallow. My doctor finally said, "Sherry, I don't know what's going on here, but the growth that was in your throat is not there now."

I just sat there and grinned. "I think I can explain it, Doctor. I had a blessing."

The tumor had shown up on the X ray. The doctors felt a growth in my throat. I could feel a growth in my throat. Then, two days later, it was gone. The only possible explanation is that it was a healing.

That incident was fourteen years ago now, and there's never been any indication of a tumor since.

Why me? I don't consider myself such a wonderful person. I think the healing was just something that He wanted to do for me at that time, possibly to strengthen my faith, I don't really know. I don't think that every blessing or prayer is always answered in exactly the way we want, but I do have such a wonderful feeling towards God that He would do such a thing for me.

From my healing, I learned that prayer is a very individual act. My own prayer was just a conversing with God, my beloved Father in heaven who loves me very dearly. The Bible says He created us in His image and likeness, so I just think of Him as a person. Given that human image of God, I think He felt my pain. I even think God has a sense of humor and laughs at some of the things I do.

If you have an illness, if you need help to get through a problem or if you need strength, all you have to do is ask for help. He's there for you.

He was there for me the next year, at the age of 40, when I received another blessing from an Elder. In the Latter-Day Saints religion you receive this blessing, a Patriarchal blessing, once in your life. Normally it's done when you're 16 or 17 but I'd become a Mormon as an adult. I had put it off even longer, though, because I thought the Elder wouldn't be able to come up with anything very positive to say when he prayed over me. I wasn't very secure. But it was time.

I had never met the Elder who gave me my blessing. All he asked me was my name, age, and the amount of time I'd been a member of the church.

He began the blessing with, "Dear sister Sherry, as Patriarch and by authority of the Holy Priesthood I lay hands upon your head and give unto you your Patriarchal blessing. This blessing will guide and be a source of comfort and understanding unto you as you continue your life in the kingdom here upon earth. Be of good cheer, for your Heavenly Father is watching over you. You are never alone and can pray at any time."

The most moving part of the blessing came later on when I heard him say, "You will be blessed with the gift of motherhood as the Lord deems fit for you to do so. And this blessing will be a great joy in your life. And you may pray to your Heavenly Father for the guidance and help that you need in this regard."

Tears just came gushing out of me when he said that. It was just so unexpected to hear this from a man who knew almost nothing about me.

Larry and I wanted to have children, but it was a bit complicated. I had been raped when I was 19, and I don't think that had ever really been resolved. My mother had called me a slut when I told her about it. Larry was also disturbed about it though he was very sympathetic towards me. There wasn't any physical reason I couldn't conceive; nonetheless, I couldn't get pregnant. So we accepted that if God wanted us to have children, we'd have them.

But as I grew older, it became more and more difficult to think about babies. I'd get upset at baby showers—or even just seeing a pregnant woman.

For three years after my blessing, I still could not conceive, but I continued to pray. Then on the 4th of July, 1985, I was shocked to discover that I was pregnant! We had a daughter, Ashley, and two years later, when I was 45, I had another daughter, Allison. I'm so thankful to God that I'm able to be a mother—to have felt something inside me grow; to see my children grow; to hear them say their prayers at night and, "Mommy, I love you."

I can't imagine life without being able to pray. I pray that God will protect Larry. I pray a lot for patience because I'm not a very patient person. When I take the kids to school I pray to the Lord that he will watch over them.

When I hear someone say that they don't believe in God and prayer, I really feel sad for them because I believe so strongly that God exists and that He does answer prayers. Being healed of cancer and becoming a mother is proof to me that prayers can be answered.

A Hostage in Iran

Yea, though I walk through the valley of the shadow of death, I will fear no evil: for thou art with me, thy rod and thy staff comfort me.

Psalms 23:4

Jerry Plotkin, a 48-year-old Los Angeles businessman, was taken hostage on November 4, 1979, in the American embassy in Tehran, Iran, by fanatical Iranians whose bloody revolution ultimately overthrew the Shah. After being held for fifteen months, he and fifty-one other hostages were released on January 20, 1981. Plotkin, a heavy-set, good-humored, graying man, is now retired and lives in Beverly Hills, California, with his wife Debbie and sons Adam, 9, and Matthew, 12. He is a recent recipient of a heart transplant.

When I went to his home to interview him, I was shown into a sunny living room where we sat and discussed our very different Iranian experiences. I had shot films there at three different times during the 70's, so I had witnessed firsthand the repression that led to the Shah's overthrow.

At the time of his kidnapping, Jerry was in Iran to meet with representatives of an Iranian copper mine and the Korean government.

When I went to the American Embassy to meet the business attaché, I saw a group of Iranians waiting in line for exit visas. I just showed my American passport and I was waved right in. It was actually an incredibly exciting time for me: There I was, a former street kid from Brooklyn telling my government that I had just concluded a very lucrative business deal for my company. I was in a great mood and was looking forward to going home.

Ten minutes later, the Iranian terrorists stormed the building and I became a hostage. The terrorists—wearing camouflage jackets and carrying weapons—were yelling and screaming and pushing us around. It was a madhouse of confusion and fear.

• • •

For the first fifty-five days, we were blindfolded and our hands and feet were tied. I was the only civilian. All of the other hostages were diplomats or military serving in the embassy. Ten of us were held in a dungeonlike room under the embassy. It was so cold down there, your spit would turn to ice before it hit the floor.

On the sixth day of captivity, after the Ayatollah (the religious leader who had replaced the Shah) approved the hostage-taking, the terrorists tied our hands and feet to our chairs, and they put cotton on our eyes underneath our blindfolds.

After a while, probably a few hours but I'm not quite sure, I heard them take one of the Americans out. A screen door slammed and then I heard Iranians screaming, angry. Minutes later I was stunned to hear a loud gunshot, then women crying and screaming. Before I even had a chance to understand what had happened, the guards stormed back in, with more yelling, and dragged another American out of the room. Another gunshot blast and more women crying.

I was terrified! I had never been so frightened in my entire life. I tried to sink down in my chair so I'd look less conspicuous.

I had never been so close to death. I just kept thinking, "Jerry, get ready to meet your maker." I couldn't think about anything—I was just so afraid.

Then, at the height of my fear, I heard an incredible voice—a voice within me. Very clearly this voice told me, "I am with you, be not afraid."

The voice startled me. I wasn't religious. I'd always believed I could take care of myself, so I never really thought much about God. As a kid in Brooklyn, my father would take me up to the roof of our building and say, "Jerry, you don't have to go to a synagogue or a church. If you want God, just look up to heaven. There's God, and He's always there." But when I heard that voice, I knew that God was with me, inside me, in my soul—connected to me. And I knew He was protecting me.

Sitting, bound to that embassy chair in the midst of all that yelling, gunfire, and crying, I experienced my very first connection with God. I was so afraid. I'd never even been overseas before this. I didn't have the mental strength to deal with a gun being aimed at my head. Nothing I'd ever done had prepared me to be a captive of religious zealots.

But when I heard, "Fear not, I am with you," I recognized God's presence, and I sat up in my chair.

• • •

I later discovered that the Americans were not actually being executed. It was a sham; the Iranians were just playing a sick mind game with us. And this madness went on all the time. Some of the hostages were brutally beaten, particularly two or three of the ranking American officials. I had gun butts smashed against my head pretty regularly. I wouldn't be able to hear for weeks afterwards. It was very painful. Also, when we were blindfolded they'd let us walk into walls or doors. I busted up my nose a few times.

So what keeps you from pooping in your pants, or breaking down and crying? Where do you muster the strength to endure? I believe you have to surrender yourself to God, to admit that, "Hey, God, I really, really need some help! What do I do, God? I don't know anything, God. It's in your hands."

• • •

The guards told us that if anyone tried to free us, they would execute everyone. So when President Carter's rescue helicopters crashed in the desert we were all hurriedly moved from the embassy basement to a jail in Shiraz. Soon after our arrival, the guards showed us films of Iraqi prisoners being executed during their war against Iraq. The Iraqis were stripped to their underwear, taken outside, and shot in the head at close range. It was a horrible thing to see but they made us watch it.

Later the same day, the guards came to my cell and made me take off all my clothes except my underwear. They blindfolded me, dragged me outside, pushing and yelling. Then I felt a gun barrel on my forehead. In that instant, time froze. I was going to die, in a dirty courtyard, thousands of miles from my home and family and . . . "Click." The sound of a firing pin. Then I heard the guards laughing, and I was taken back to my cell.

• • •

We never knew what the guards were going to do or how long we would be held. One night I became overwhelmingly depressed. I can't remember what month or day it was. Before then, I'd never really thought of suicide. I'd always felt that somehow I'd get back to my wife and family. I got down on my knees in the darkness, on that jail floor, and I reached out to God. I wanted to feel His presence and to know what I should do. I prayed, but not in what I thought of as the traditional sense. I felt I had a very special one-on-one relationship with God, so I spoke out loud: "Help me, God, give me the strength to handle this ordeal. Please, God, don't let me weaken, let me be a man." A figure appeared to me in that dark jail cell, shrouded in white. When I saw it, I knew that God was with me and that He'd answered my prayer.

• • •

One day one of the guards opened the cell door and threw a Bible at me. I opened it to a passage that said something like, "Go among the people and speak against the barbarians." So on the occasion when Iranian TV came by for interviews, I tried to speak my mind although most of my speech was censored. (Since I was the only civilian hostage, I wasn't under the same constraints as the soldiers and embassy employees.) My comments gave my family a chance to see that I was alive and in good shape.

• • •

When we were finally set free and our plane took off for the States, I remember standing up to see my fellow hostages. "Well, it's nice to finally meet all of you!" I said. I had actually only come into contact with seven of the fifty-one other hostages during the siege.

After I returned home and saw my family, my wife and I were brought to West Point to meet President Reagan. I couldn't believe that I was going to meet the President! I was so thankful. I looked up at the sky, at the gorgeous white clouds, at the beautiful Hudson River. There was snow on the ground and on the trees. I looked to the heavens and I said, "Please, God, tell me, what should I do?" Just as I had on that day when I thought I was going to be killed, the first time I spoke to God. God's voice came to me again, and His answer was so simple. He said two words to me: "Do good."

I realized He meant that in your daily life, all you really have to do is to do good. To your family, to your friends, to your coworkers, and to your loved ones. And if you follow this simple message, you can fulfill yourself and all those around you.

• • •

For five years after the ordeal, I met with my fellow hostages to insure the Marines and embassy people were compensated for their incarceration. I wasn't financially compensated because I was a civilian, but I wanted to do good for those who needed help. So together we raised education money for the children of those eight brave young men who lost their lives trying to rescue us in the U.S. military helicopter operation.

At first, after I came home, I hated my captors. But that hatred soon disappeared. I didn't have time or room for that emotion. I've got too much to be grateful for now. The guards were just young guys. Sometimes when their superiors weren't around, they'd show me pictures of their kids. In a way, they were hostages too, victims of the Ayatollah and his madness.

"There are no atheists in foxholes" is an old adage which rings very true for me. If a person has been exposed to Buddha, God, Allah, or whatever god you choose, you realize that sometimes there are no human answers. So you look for spiritual answers. After you've received God, or God has received you and you know you are at one with God, you find yourself freer, without the limitations you'd previously held yourself to. I knew I could achieve whatever I set my mind to, and I went out and did it. At one point recently, I was devastated when a business venture failed. But I very quickly got up, brushed myself off and started all over again—and became successful. I didn't do it alone: I had the spirit of God with me.

Occasionally I give talks to people about my months as a hostage. I try to give them the message that when they go through life they should never, never give up. I want people to know that God is with you during harrowing times. You're really not alone. And then when the crisis is over, you can walk into a room and look at your friends and say, "I didn't crack!" You'll know it was God's presence that enabled you to overcome.

Given the challenges I've had to deal with, I shouldn't even be here. Between living through the danger in Iran, recovering from the loss of almost everything I had during my captivity, and most recently, surviving my heart transplant (not to mention finding a heart donor in two weeks when some people wait up to two years for one), I have plenty of proof that God is taking care of me. I really believe He has something more for me to do, that I have another purpose in life. That's why I believe in God. Because I'm still here!

Breaking One of the Ten Commandments

He that hath my commandments, and keepeth them, he it is that loveth me: and he that loveth me shall be loved of my father, and I will love him, and manifest myself to him.

John 14:21

Kevin Colder is a 38-year-old chief petty officer in the United States Navy. Born in Chester, Pennsylvania, he was seven years old when he and his brother were put into a foster home after his mother was incarcerated for check forgery. Kevin was later raised by his grandmother as well as his single mother. After a minor brush with the law, he joined the Navy when he was twenty years old. The best man at his wedding gave Kevin a book of the Koran, which led to his eight years as a member of The Black Muslim religion. He then returned to the Christian worship he was brought up with as a child.

Kevin is a Religious Programs Specialist at the Camp Pendleton, California, Marine Base where I talked to him. A handsome, agile man, Kevin was immaculately dressed in his uniform. He spoke rapidly with hand movements that emphasized his story. Kevin, the base racquetball champion, is married and has two teenage sons.

Around 1990 or so my relationship with my wife DeAnne was getting strained. I couldn't discuss anything that was on my mind; personal stuff, financial stuff, my job. My inability to talk about these problems was destroying us and I began to think about other women.

One day, I was on my way to work on Highway 5, listening to a gospel tape in my car, when I saw her. A woman driving next to me beckoned me with a wave of her hand. She pulled over, and I stopped to see what she wanted. As she walked towards me I thought, "My God, look at that woman!" In a matter of seconds I yanked my tape out of the cassette player and pushed it under the seat, pulled off my wedding ring and put it in my pocket. I turned my whole life inside out without even thinking!

I read somewhere in the Bible that God would give you a good woman if you prayed. I did pray for that while I was growing up and in the midst of all my problems He put DeAnne in my life. You couldn't find a finer woman or a more beautiful mother, but after eighteen years of marriage I was attracted to this other woman. After a few encounters I started having an affair with her.

DeAnne and I were both attending Faith Temple Christian Center. The kids were in Sunday school and I was in the choir. During the service I would go to altar call for repentance. I would plead for God to forgive me for sinning. I wanted the Lord to forgive me, but I didn't want to change. I didn't have the courage to face my adultery. It was like I was on drugs, but my drug was sex.

In the beginning I didn't think the affair would last long. DeAnne would never know or suspect. But I was wrong. The other woman knew I was married, but she didn't care. At first, I didn't know how to get out of it, and then I convinced myself it was something I wanted.

When I was with my wife I would often think about the other woman. And I'd think of DeAnne when I was with the other woman. It was a no-win situation, and it was driving me nuts!

Finally, it came to a head. An aunt died in Florida and I went there alone—without DeAnne and the kids—for the funeral. I told her I was going to stay down there a few days after the funeral, but I actually made plans with this other woman to come right back and stay with her.

During this time the problems in Somalia were coming to a head, and the base chaplain called DeAnne in order to get in touch with me in Florida. DeAnne called my relatives, who told her I had already left. Later I called her and lied and said I was still in Florida and to tell my boss that I was returning.

When I did come home, I came straight out and told DeAnne what I was doing. I was just tired of lying to her. Because our relationship was so strained already, I guess I didn't think it would devastate her. But I was wrong.

DeAnne wanted to get a divorce.

During the few weeks before I left for Somalia, she flip-flopped about it; wanting a divorce, then not wanting a divorce. I didn't know what I wanted. Neither did she.

But I was praying daily for the Lord to show me how to resolve the mess I was in. I read a book titled *How to Love Your Wife.* It said that Christ wants us to exemplify him to the nth degree. Christ is the Father, the priest, and the saint, and as a husband that's what I was supposed to be to my wife. And in the Scripture I read that if I didn't repent, truly repent, I was going to hell. The word "re-pent" just kept hitting me.

In Somalia my job as a Religious Programs Specialist was to arrange the schedules for all the chaplain's services. I'm also a bodyguard for the chaplain. My job is administrative but I really feel I'm a disciple, so I prayed constantly for the success of the chaplain's program. In some parts of Somalia, I was putting my life on the line.

I saw pictures of Somalia before the fighting, and it was tranquil and beautiful. When we got there it was all blown up and destroyed. The university was ravaged. People were living like animals in mud huts, the kids were sick, and there was the constant threat of shooting and death.

The Somalis were all Muslims. I invited some of them to our services and we all prayed together. It was wonderful and very moving.

After I'd been in Somalia for two weeks, my wife sent a message through the Red Cross requesting I come home. But the division chaplain said he couldn't let me go because I was the senior chief petty officer. He told me to try talking to my wife.

She told me she'd left her job and was on the verge of a nervous breakdown. In the midst of all the death, destruction, and chaos in Somalia I was being torn apart by the realization of what I'd done to my wife and to our marriage back home. I was an adulterer.

I prayed not only for me and my wife but also for the Somalis and our troops. I did a lot of conversing with the Lord during the time I was in Somalia. If you don't talk to Him, He doesn't hear what you need. I don't think it's enough to only think prayers. You have to speak out loud to God.

"Not my will but thine be done," it says in the Bible. My will had committed adultery, and I had broken one of the Ten Commandments. I never really thought my wife and I were going to get back together because of the damage I had done. But I prayed to God for guidance. "Knock and the door shall open," the Bible tells us. And man, was I knocking!

When I got back to the States after my tour of duty, I cried when I first saw my wife, DeAnne: I literally broke down myself. She had lost weight and looked miserable. The pain in her was so evident it tore my heart out. I told God I would never, ever get involved with another woman again. At the time I didn't realize that when I told her about the affair, it was the beginning of my process of repenting. I believe the Lord took me away from my wife to Somalia so that I could really see what I had done.

No one should ever inflict that kind of pain on another human being, especially not to a saint like DeAnne. My wife was a child of God. The day I returned I made up my mind that I was going to repent. When we went to church on Sunday I immediately went to the altar and truly, completely gave my life to the Lord. And I heard His voice say, "I forgive you." I said, "Lord, thank you."

When I knew the Lord had forgiven me, it didn't matter what happened between DeAnne and me. It didn't matter what other people thought. I can never forget that I committed adultery but it's not part of me anymore. I believe it when He says He forgives us for our sins. And after we have been cleansed and forgiven we can be healed.

So DeAnne and I went to Christian counseling, and we both prayed that God would show us the right thing to do about our marriage. It was a year of days and nights of praying and arguments. It was an experience that I'm now grateful for, but I never want to go through it again.

I learned that when you turn your face from the Lord and sin, you are actually turning your back on Christ. Then He can't do anything for you until you return to Him and repent. And when you ask Him to help you, He truly will.

I know that the devil tests us with temptations. And he gets upset every time someone accepts the Lord in his life. You've got to put on the full armor of God to protect yourself. You've got to get into the Scripture, and as you do that, your armor gets stronger and thicker.

Lots of religions and preachers insist that we are all sinners. I believe that we all sin, but God forgives us and loves us, and if you are a child of God, a Christian, and believe in Jesus Christ, and repent your sin, I believe you are healed.

My prayers were answered, my marriage is whole again; and I thank God every single day for my wonderful wife, my sons, and my marriage. If someone who had been committing adultery was sitting next to me now and wanted to repent, I would take his hand and ask him to pray with me:

"Father, God, in the name of Jesus, this person is hurting right now. Please give him the strength to look at you, Lord, and say 'Please forgive me and grant the repentance you have promised.' Father, God, as he repents in his heart, please manifest in his life the benefits you have promised us through Jesus Christ. Holy Spirit, I want you right now to move in our lives and with the grace and power of God make us love Christ. Father, God, I just want to thank you for healing my life right now. Devil, I'm serving you notice right now that you are under our feet and that you have no way, no way, in this house. I just ask you, child of God, do you truly repent? Tell Christ, tell God, in your own words that you confess your sins, and then ask for forgiveness. Father, God, accept this prayer in Jesus' name. Thank you for the power and the strength and the courage to do what is right. Amen."

The Jacksonville Twirling Academy

It is God Himself who prays through us, when we pray to Him. . . . We cannot bridge the gap between God and ourselves even through the most intensive and frequent prayers; the gap between God and ourselves can only be bridged by God.

Paul Tillich

Norma Deering is a lifelong resident of Jacksonville, Florida, and has been married to Peter, a circuit judge, for 22 years. For six years she has been a prayer minister at Christian Healing Ministries in Jacksonville, an interdenominational ministry that teaches and practices healing prayer.

Norma, 42, is the mother of five children, ages 17 to 27. She is a stylishly dressed, attractive blonde who personifies the healthy, suntanned Florida look.

As we talked in her spacious office, it wasn't hard to envision this lively woman as the cheerleader and baton twirler that she once was. Her soft, Southern accent complements her considerable enthusiasm for God, family, and church.

I remember the first time I actually heard what I now know was the voice of God. I was seven years old, and a voice distinctly said to me, "You need to go to your parents and tell them what's happening to you." I had been sexually molested by a teenage neighbor since the age of five.

When I told my parents that I was being molested, they believed me, the boy was confronted, and it was stopped. That was the first time that God, the Holy Spirit, spoke to me and freed me from a damaging experience.

My Baptist parents were both born on small farms in Tennessee and worked very hard all their lives. They were moral people, but we didn't go to church a lot. I felt a lot of "hellfire and brimstone" condemnation at their church, and I really didn't have a spiritual, loving upbringing. Although I knew there was a God, I always felt that He was often angry with me.

In grade school and high school I was very active in baton twirling. I was good at it, and for many years that was my God. I was perceived as the stereotypical dumb blonde, airhead majorette. My belief that men only looked at me as a physical person, combined with the memories of my being molested, resulted in my feeling empty and unloved while growing up.

After graduating from high school, I thought court reporting was something I could do, so I enrolled in a local school to learn this profession. I believed that if I got the right job, made a lot of money, had a sports car and lots of nice, wealthy guys to date, I'd have a sense of self-worth. I remember walking around downtown Jacksonville during class breaks, feeling very lonely and confused, wondering what I was really looking for.

"Pause a While to Pray Today" was the sign on the front of a Methodist Church I used to visit after school.

Even though I'd go there to pray, I really didn't know how to back then. I longed for someone to come up to me on the street and tell me, "Here's what you're seeking. Let me tell you about my relationship with the Lord." But it never happened.

Then one day I met Peter, a law clerk, downtown. He was 25, divorced, and had twin three-year-old girls and a boy, five. He was living with his parents, who were helping him raise the children. I was very attracted to him but I remember thinking I didn't want to get involved with somebody who was divorced and had three kids.

One night soon after I had met him, I was in bed praying for God to fill this emptiness or loneliness or whatever it was in me and I absolutely, positively heard God tell me, "Peter is the man I want you to marry."

"But, God, wait a minute. He's divorced. He's got three kids. I don't know anything about being a mother. I've got my whole life ahead of me!"

"Yes, I know," God said to me.

"Fine." I answered Him sort of flippantly. "If you want me to marry Peter, you will have to deal with my mother." She was a very protective, divorce-hating Baptist mother.

Well, He did deal with her, and at the age of 20 I became a wife and an instant mother to three little kids.

What I saw in Peter I never saw in anyone else. I saw Jesus, and it drew me to him like a magnet. Peter was raised in a home with total, unconditional love, a nurturing home where you were loved even more when you messed up than when you didn't. He led me to his church, St. Peter's Episcopal Church; to his father, an Episcopal priest for 53 years; and most importantly, to the Lord.

Peter also loved me spiritually, in an unconditionally accepting way that I'd always wanted.

• • •

I'd opened the Jacksonville Baton Twirling Academy when I was 18 years old. I had about 50 students when I was a court reporter, and when I quit reporting after I married, the school grew and grew. My plan was to make it the largest in the U.S. I worked towards that goal, expanding, franchising, teaching, traveling and judging baton-twirling contests.

Even though I went to church on Sunday and had filled some of the financial and family holes in my life, I worshipped my business. I realized my baton-twirling school gave me feelings of being accepted and a sense of prestige and respect. I was bowing down to a lot of false Gods.

So my prayer of surrender became, "Lord, here I am again, making a mess of it. God, this is what I want to do, now please bless it and stamp your approval on it." I now realize I was trying to do Norma's will in His name. But it doesn't work that way, it works God's way.

One Sunday I was on my knees sobbing at the altar in church when I told God, "If my baton-twirling school separates me from you, I'll give it to you. I've made this school my God, and I repent." I knew that Jesus should be the Lord of my life—not my business.

After that I began to hear Him again. In truth, I began to listen instead of talking. The Lord told me, "I appreciate that you want to give me this baton school, but this is what I'm going to do. I'll be the owner and you'll be the manager."

At that time I had worked up to about 300 students with 15 girls working for me. Very quickly, almost effortlessly, the school started growing.

People in the business began to wonder why my school was growing so much so I wrote a few articles explaining that I had turned my school over to Jesus Christ. Then people thought I was crazy.

I gradually gave little pieces of my life to the Lord. First it was my marriage, then the kids and finally the baton school.

• • •

The turning point in my prayer life came in 1981. My son Jason was six years old and in the first grade. I was growing as a Christian, trying to give different areas of my life to the Lord. Jason wasn't getting his work done in school, and I kept getting notes from his teacher saying he was daydreaming, looking out the window, and was easily distracted.

Does God care about small stuff, I wondered. Is prayer just for important things like cancer, unemployment, and war? Is God too busy to deal with little things?

I decided to experiment with prayer for this problem with Jason. I wasn't going to tell anyone, not even Jason or my family. It was just between me and Jesus. I prayed for Jason every day for about a month.

Then one day I was washing dishes in the kitchen and talking to my friend Beth. She asked me how I heard God's voice. I told her that sometimes when you read Scripture something just jumps off the page for you, or a sermon in church touches your heart in a special way.

While we were talking, Jason rushed in from school and got a Popsicle out of the freezer. He heard our conversation and he pulled on my skirt and said, "Mommy, sometimes I hear Jesus' voice."

"When does this happen?" I asked him.

"Mommy, I hear Jesus' voice at school when I'm not getting my work done," he said. "When I'm looking out the window Jesus says to me, 'C'mon, Jason, let's get this school work finished. You can do it.' "

That day I knew without reservation that God had time to take care of everything. The Lord was saying to me, "If it's important to you, Norma, it's important to me. If you'll give it to me, talk to me about it, I will move. I'll be there. Trust me." I began to pray about everything and have continued to do so ever since that day!

Soon after that I got interested in physical healing through prayer. Can people really lay hands on the sick, like Jesus did, and heal? I wondered.

I began to pray for the kids when they had a headache or were hurt in a football game. The more I saw that my prayers were answered, the more encouraged I became, and I prayed for more and more people.

In 1985, after a lot of praying, I decided to sell my baton-twirling school and become a full-time prayer minister.

Initially when I started praying for people, I got confused because some people I prayed for would be healed and others wouldn't. I finally learned my job was to pray, His was to heal. Sometimes He heals right away, while other times it might take a few years, or He may end someone's pain with death. I don't understand it all, but I have to accept that. All I know is that my job is to pray and I love doing it.

My prayer is often, "Lord, empty me out and let me be a drainpipe, open at the top and the bottom. Let me lay hands on people and you pour your power through me to them."

• • •

One night my seven-year-old son Danny had come running into the house very pale and scared. He had gone through the woods with his sisters to see some horses. "Why aren't you with Shelly and Mandy?" I asked.

"I was being naughty so they told me to come home," Danny said.

"Well, what's wrong?" I asked him.

"They thought I knew the way home but I really didn't. I was real scared. But I just kept saying, 'Jesus will show me the way. Jesus will show me the way,' and Mommy, He did."

I'd say that's a pretty good description of what Jesus has done for me in my life as well.

The Medicine Man

How can we have confidence in white people? When Jesus Christ came upon the earth, you killed him and nailed him to a cross. You thought he was dead and you were mistaken.

Tecumseh, Shawnee Chief

Native American Jasper Thomas Garrett ("J.T.") is a Cherokee medicine man. He attended Western Carolina University on a scholarship and received a bachelor's degree, majoring in biology and business administration. He also has a master's and a doctorate in public health. A Vietnam veteran, J.T. is presently an administrator at the Cherokee Indian Hospital in Cherokee, N.C.

J.T.'s father was Irish and his mother was a mixed-blood Cherokee. When I interviewed this affable 55-year-old man, he was dressed in a button-down white shirt, tan slacks, and wing tip shoes. Around his neck he wore a large necklace of colorful beads woven into a unique Indian design.

I've made films on the Navajos and the Oglala Sioux and understand Native Americans' reticence in talking with white people. After I made numerous requests to a variety of Native Americans to talk about prayer, J.T. was the first to agree to an interview.

Our visit began with J.T. saying a Cherokee prayer.

In the Indian world, everything starts and ends with a prayer. In English, my prayer means, "Oh, Great One, I'm thankful I have the time to give this man. And I'm grateful for you, Great One, that you are with me." We think of prayer as a circle that we come into.

The reason a lot of Native Americans won't talk to outsiders is because many tribes have been devastated by the white man's laws. We have an oral tradition of passing stories from one generation to the next, but when stories are passed along, Indians are always told, "Keep them to yourselves or the white man will take them and you will have no power." Our power, simply put, is our spiritual existence.

In spite of these traditions, Indians are willing to let me talk, because they know I will honor the traditions and respect everything that is in the medicine. Part of my mission is to help others understand that traditional Indian medicine is not a dinosaur of the past. It's a very dynamic part of our lives today.

My grandfather was a very strong spiritual person. He practiced the medicine and taught me to learn it as well. The definition of the word "medicine" for Native Americans is all the things that encompass our lives. In Cherokee we say "nuwahtee," meaning a form of medicine that is an energy.

At the reservation school I attended as a child I pulled away from anybody who wanted to study the medicine. I only wanted to be the most popular kid and the best athlete. But my name, Jasper, comes from the Jasper stone, and my grandmother always told me that it was a healing stone. Somehow, I knew deep down inside that I would end up studying the medicine and learning the spiritual ways of our people.

• • •

In 1974 something inside me said to go on a vision quest. A vision quest is a spiritual journey in which you seek a vision of your future, your role in life, your purpose. In the Cherokee way we call it "spiraling," moving to another level. I discussed it with a medicine man and then went up into the mountains for three days.

I took my medicine pouch and shared tobacco with mother earth. I didn't eat, and I said simple prayers. "I am here. I am open and I ask for guidance."

Most of what happened there is sacred to me. Later, I described my vision to the medicine man. In it, I was bridging the gap, helping everybody—regardless of language, color, or creed—to better understand that we are all here for a single purpose. I didn't know what this meant right away.

In 1975 I was the coordinator for safety and industrial hygiene for the Bendix Corporation in Michigan. I was a young guy off the reservation, with a wonderful wife and two little kids. I wore a three-piece suit and traveled around in a company jet. Although my lifestyle was rather conventional, on several occasions, Native American elders told me it was time to take up the medicine.

I was, and still am, a member of the United Methodist Church, but at that time the church didn't completely meet my spiritual needs. I also struggled with the idea that if I wasn't a full-blood Indian I couldn't go into the medicine. I was a little afraid of the whole idea, yet every time I saw anything that reminded me of my grandfather, like a rock at the river's edge, I would sense a connection with the medicine.

One day, about a year after my vision quest, I got a call from a medicine man asking me to come and visit. So I went down to the Cherokee reservation in North Carolina to see him. When I arrived at his home, his back was turned to me.

I said, "Hey, I'm here and ready to talk to you."

He didn't say anything and we just sat there for 45 minutes. Then he eased around and said, "You are not ready."

"What do you mean, I'm not ready? You're the one calling me. I came all the way down here to give up my career?" I was a little rude to the elder.

"Well, go back home and I will come to you."

Back at home, my wife told me she had had a dream: She was on an elevator. It stopped and a man in a plaid shirt with a hat got on. Although she had never met him, she knew he was the medicine man I had visited. "It's going to be okay," he told her.

Several years later, in the middle of a bad Michigan winter, my little boy and I were driving on an interstate when we saw a car go off the highway. There were other cars on and off the road. One car struck another one and ended up on top of the car it hit.

I was trying to keep my car on the slippery road, but I saw a man's body project out of the car and then go back in. My son said, "Look, Dad, do you see that man going through the windshield?" I found myself praying, "Oh, Great One, let this man live. And now it's time for me to go home."

What I prayed must have been floating around in me

for a while, but it took an incident like that horrible car crash to bring it out. I knew at that instant I would go home to the Smoky Mountains and be a medicine man.

Still, I was careful to keep things to myself. Imagine someone sitting in my office at Bendix asking me what I wanted to do, and me saying, "Well, I want to go back to the Cherokee reservation to be a medicine man."

The car accident was in 1978 and we moved shortly thereafter because I was hired as the administrator at the Cherokee Indian Hospital in North Carolina, which gave me financial stability while I learned the medicine.

Seven different medicine men taught me. A Natchez from Oklahoma told me, "My people hold some of the medicine that was passed on to the Cherokee. To help you bridge the gap, I have some prayer chants and ceremonies for you from my family." A medicine woman taught me the use of herbs. I'd already learned a lot of that from my mother, who showed me how to draw energy from a plant and how to use it.

In the traditional way, energy is universal and is connected to everything else. We think of a tree as being a protective energy. Water is a healing energy. One of the energies we tend to misunderstand the most and use the least is the energy of prayer. It's humble energy when you address the Great One, but boy, is it powerful!

In the Native American way, prayer energy is not selfish energy. You give thanks for things. You pray for something, or someone—your brother or sister. Medicine is a way of life that includes the mental, physical, natural, and spiritual. We think illness starts with the spirit, not the body. You have to have balance and harmony as in the medicine wheel, the circle.

Prayer is an everyday part of Indian life. We don't segregate it into time frames or occasions or rituals. It's simply a way of life. Prayer is giving thanks to the Great One. This brings peace of mind and healing.

I have no problems saying "God." After all, I am a Christian. But I feel better saying "Great One." When I say Great One, I'm talking about universal spirit. We have so many choices out there, we should go for what works.

I tell people all the time, "I am not a healer or a shaman of some mystical past. I'm a teacher, a helper. It's the other person that makes me a medicine man." I'm a spiritual helper, in that I help clarify what's going on. Sometimes it's hard, sometimes it's soft. I listen, I repeat, I mirror things back.

• • •

One day, during my training, an elder visited me at my office in the hospital. "There are some things you haven't learned. Like the blessing way," he said.

"What am I supposed to learn?" I asked.

"If I teach you, you won't learn it. You must seek it out and find it yourself."

He was a great elder, and people were a little afraid of him because of all of his energy. I was honored by his visit. He left a rock on my desk.

Later that day, a woman asked me to give a talk to some of the kids in the hospital about seeking things. I said, "Wow, what a coincidence. I was just talking to somebody about that."

I went up to the nearby mountains to think. I found myself picking up rocks of all sizes and shapes. I was suddenly thankful for this rock and that one, and so on.

When I did speak to the children in the hospital, I told

them that Mother Nature had all kinds of special things, blessings for us. All we had to do was seek them out and be sure to be thankful for what she provides. A few days later a little girl gave me a rock in the shape of a heart. "You must have found this in Mother Nature," I said.

She agreed and said, "I'm giving it to you."

"What did you leave the Earth Mother?" I asked.

She smiled and said, "I told her you would take care of that."

The connection with the rocks and the child helped me understand the meaning of blessings, which is giving thanks. If you learn to appreciate the rock as an energy, and we all share that energy, we are all kin. I have to teach young people their blessing ways, to give thanks and to learn the value of all things. "You can't be a teacher unless you learn," the elder told me.

My spirituality is a combination of my Native American spirit ways and my Christianity. It's part of my role as a bridge. If we have good medical technology, let's utilize it. If it doesn't work, let's go the spirit way. If a person can't live in the physical, let's help him live in the spirit. It's all interconnected.

I went to a conference where a man who studied the Mayan calendar said that when you reach the age of 52, you can start over. I accepted that idea and decided to start over. Now I don't have to carry the baggage of being a mixed breed, or worry about whether I'm accepted, or what I look like. I can wear my beads or not wear my beads. For the first time in my life I can say to myself I'm a helper, and I can help other people heal. That's powerful.

I don't have any hard feelings against the white man. I had a white father, a good man, whom I loved very much.

The Cherokee way teaches us that we have to come together, and when we do that, there is forgiveness. In the best sense of religion and spirituality, there is a cleansing. There has to be cleansing for what was done in the past to Native Americans.

One of the basic beliefs of Indians is that they are the keepers of the earth. If we could learn to respect everything, we wouldn't have to make excuses for the harm that has been done to the earth and its people. We could include everyone in our prayers to the Great One and say thank you.

Learning to Be Brave

The most beautiful thing we can experience is the mysterious. It is the source of all true art and science.

Albert Einstein

Elizabeth Star, the oldest of four daughters of a Methodist minister father, was born in Arizona and grew up in Northern California. After thirty years of marriage she divorced her husband and quit her job. She is now traveling the United States in a 22-foot Winnebago on what she describes as a trip of spiritual discovery. I interviewed Elizabeth in San Antonio, Texas, where she was staying with a friend during a pause in her trip. Tall, slim, and wearing a denim dress, she enthusiastically talked of her life on the road.

At the end of my interview, Elizabeth thanked me for the opportunity to talk with me. "I've never really talked at one time about my life. It's been helpful for me to do this." Several months after our interview she sent me a typed, single-spaced, five-page letter, clarifying the discussion we had had in Texas.

One day I was gardening in my backyard in San Diego,

California. I was married to a very successful medical doctor at the time. We had a lovely home, we traveled, we were churchgoers. On the surface, we had an ideal life. But I wasn't happy. The Cuban missile crisis was in the news, my marriage was difficult, and I felt empty and purposeless inside.

I remember sitting in the garden thinking, "I've got to know who the only begotten son of God is, because only He can save us from blowing ourselves and the world up."

Suddenly I felt like I was going into an altered state. I was watering the garden, pulling weeds, but I really wasn't there! I sensed a very strong presence. A voice vibrated in my head but I felt it outside of me too. The words seemed to reverberate in every cell of my body as if it was an electrical impulse.

A strong, clear male voice in my head said, "If you would test Jesus, would you be willing to hold up your end by doing what he asks?"

It seemed only fair that I respond, "Yes."

"Thou shalt love the Lord your God with all your heart, with all your mind, and with all your strength," the voice said.

"But, how can I love something I can't see or feel?" I asked.

"That is your life challenge" was the response.

Then I asked, "Did you say *all* my mind?"

"Yes!"

"I can ask any question, go anyplace, like to a Buddhist temple or to a psychic, to learn the truth?"

"Yes," my messenger replied. "But it's important that you keep your hand in mine."

It was as if all the walls enclosing my mind had crashed

around me. I felt at peace. Jesus, Buddha, Mohammed, me and my husband, we were all the Begotten Son. That was my answer. Before, I had an empty feeling in the pit of my stomach—one I could never fill. After that experience, the void was filled. I cried for three days and nights.

• • •

One of the major breakthroughs after that garden experience was the introduction into my life of the creative process, both as a means of transformation, and as a way to reach the creative God within me.

I began to work with children and adults both in the church and in the community in various programs. I always felt I was guided by God as to where to go, and what to do, and all my efforts were enormously successful.

I couldn't get enough to read, to experience, to know. I was like a starving person faced with many things to eat. I became part of prayer groups, of healing groups, and an experimental discussion group made up of women from different churches. It all blew open my perception of reality.

I had grown up in a very religious family. Later I taught Sunday school and was president of the Women's Society. But there was never a sense of authenticity to what I was doing. I grew up feeling the world was falling apart and I should have been doing something about it, but I didn't quite believe the church had the power to save the world.

I never really planned my life, but I was willing to listen, and this was part of the commitment I made during that peak experience in the garden. Whatever I was guided to do, I would follow to the best of my ability, with the faith Jesus would prove himself to me.

• • •

I did eventually get divorced, and I enrolled in Antioch University's Holistic Studies program in San Francisco. One day I was cleaning my apartment and suddenly I saw Jesus up in the corner, a very, very small apparition. I said, "There you are!" It had taken so long for him to appear, I'd begun to wonder if I'd ever see him.

He explained, "I had to become small and outside of you so that you could develop a Christ within yourself."

I realized that I had always seen the Christ as being "out there," not something close to me, or a part of me. But I knew then that the power of Christ Jesus was alive and was in me. He was a reality, I could contact him, and I wanted him to be my teacher and role model. I also knew it was time to leave my old life as I had known it.

Although I had a lovely house, a great neighborhood, and wonderful friends, I knew I had to leave it all behind. "Not my will but thine be done," it says in the Bible. I didn't know where I would go or what I would do, but I sold my house. In the midst of a bad real estate market, it sold in four days for the asking price.

Part of my transition was my claiming an integrity that I hadn't previously claimed. It meant examining all my beliefs and relationships and not supporting a government I felt was destroying America. Although I felt I was being divinely led, I was very concerned about what I was doing. And I became frightened. One of the tools by which we are controlled is fear, so I prayed, "Dear God, am I doing the right thing?"

I had finished my studies in San Francisco and moved back to San Diego, where I was a director of a nonprofit organization. A meeting was postponed so I walked to a post office, and as I passed a small used car lot a blue twenty-two-foot van drove into the lot. Something inside of me said, "That's my van!"

I bought it, stored some of my belongings with a friend and started my trip north to attend a meeting about psychotronics, which is a new technology about the mind and electronics.

The van broke down in San Jose, California, and by the time I had replaced the engine I decided to go to Mount Shasta, Washington. I spent an incredible summer there parked in my van, reading, listening, and praying. This is what my life is all about now. It's about prayer and where I'm being led by God.

I'm also learning to be brave, to live simply, and to trust. When I left San Diego a friend told me, "So you're running away from home?"

"No," I told her, "I'm very happy with my family and friends. I'm running to something and I need to free myself to reach that goal."

I have a great sense of freedom now, a sense that I'm always meeting the person I need to meet.

• • •

I can't function without prayer. That would be like trying to race down a road with only three wheels on your car. I'm in constant prayer. Prayer is my life. It's part of being whole.

My family prayer had a great influence on me. Every morning after breakfast we had prayers and Bible readings before school. I grew up with a mother who required absolute truth, love, and unselfishness.

The Bible gives reassurance. The 23rd Psalm says, "Yea, though I walk through the valley of the shadow of death, I will fear no evil." I pray that "not my will but thine be done," and I know as long as I stay in that flow—and I pray for the courage and fortitude to stay in that flow—I'll be led to do what God wants me to do.

Communicating beyond this sensual dimension of understanding is my concept of prayer. It could mean talking to an extraterrestrial, or talking to my higher self, which is on a much higher frequency, or even talking to my subconscious. It could be working with the light, with no words at all, but just knowing the light and the healing that can come with it. That's prayer, that's life, real life, which is beyond the sensual dimension.

Prayer for me is also the creative process, a process of life. Meditating has taught me how to go into the alpha or delta state, as deep as I can. That's also prayer for me, because I'm putting my mind into synchronicity, into a coherence so I can respond to God. And in doing so, things happen.

What I always hope to accomplish when I pray is to go into silence because words are so superficial. I generally relax the body, as it's part of the prayer process of using the mind, body, and emotions.

My sojourn is teaching me the art of prayer, in that it's putting my life on the line with no expectations except that my decision to lead a surrendered life will be honored and supported without my having to ask for help. A mind far greater than mine is teaching me and showing me a greater reality of God and His love for me. I think my trip itself is prayer.

I believe God is on a frequency so high that I can't even begin to comprehend or to reach it. God is like a hologram that helps me, and I'm a dot within that hologram, therefore I contain everything God contains.

I feel that I'm a spiritual warrior here to serve our nation and the planet. I'm fighting a different kind of a war, a holy war, a battle for creativity. Part of my traveling now is that I'm waiting for orders. Where I'll be led and why I'm where I am is beginning to be revealed to me through prayer. "Not my will but thine be done." It's all very exciting!

Tommy

Because he hath set his love upon me, therefore will I deliver him: I will set him on high, because he hath known my name.

He shall call upon me, and I will answer him: I will be with him in trouble: I will deliver him, and honour him.

Psalms 91:14–15

June Fay was born in Dorchester, Massachusetts, in 1940. Her parents were often on welfare and her father was an alcoholic. After high school she became a beautician and in 1965 married a Boston fireman. They had four daughters and a son. In 1977 June's husband died of a heart attack on the kitchen floor of their home in Randolph, Massachusetts.

June is a short, sturdy woman with closely cropped blonde hair who speaks rapidly in a Boston accent. Her zeal for life, her family, and God is endless and she enthusiastically shared it with me when I interviewed her at the Sacred Heart Catholic Church in Watertown.

June told me about receiving the telephone call that every mother fears; her 15½-year-old son Tommy was injured and had been taken to a hospital emergency room.

I was raised Catholic and I always believed in God, but believing in Him and knowing Him are two different things. I've been asthmatic all my life, and in 1989 I heard about a priest who was throwing water on people and knocking them down and then they were healed. I didn't believe it could be true. But I decided to see for myself.

My sister and I went to some of the healing Masses. Father McDonaugh would pray for sick people and sure enough, when he put his hands on them, they'd fall down. I thought they were weirdos and I couldn't understand why they were praising the Lord and raising their hands. But I liked the way Father McDonaugh prayed and I did feel that God was getting to me and finally opening my eyes. I realized there was more to God than I knew, more to life than I knew. So for six months I went to the healing services and then I was baptized by Father McDonaugh. Now I was one of the weirdos!

I figured that one of those healing priests would heal me of my asthma. I was at the church so often that eventually, I was asked to volunteer my time to help run the services. I didn't exactly have the best attitude, though. I said, "I'm coming here to get healed. I come to fall down, not to help."

So a priest reminded me that Abraham was told that if he did God's work, all that belonged to him would be taken care of. I started saying my rosary and soon I was really hooked on it. Ultimately, I didn't find God; He found me.

And God was certainly with me that late night in September 1990 when my phone rang. A girl told me my son Tommy had been hurt in a fight and was being taken to Boston Hospital. I immediately called the hospital but they had no record of a Tommy Fay there.

When my son left the house that night he said he was

going to a party. The two boys he was with were 18 and 19 years old, so I reminded them that Tommy was 15½ and he was not allowed to drink. I really didn't want him to go because I didn't know the kids, but my daughter Mary told me it was time to stop babying Tommy. So I let him go to the party.

Ten minutes after I called Boston Hospital they called back to say that Tommy had just been admitted. He was badly hurt and they wanted me to come right away. In a state of shock, I picked up my rosary and started praying.

When I got the hospital, Tommy was just lying there unconscious in the emergency room. He'd been badly beaten on the head. There was a lot of drinking at the party, and apparently a fight had started and Tommy tried to make some peace. As it was told to me, one kid punched Tommy and knocked him down against a tree, then another boy named George came running out of the house with a baseball bat yelling, "I'm gonna kill somebody!" He beat Tommy's head in while everyone there just stood around and watched.

I went to the hospital chapel and prayed for seven hours while the doctors operated on Tommy. He had such a severe blood clot in his head they didn't think he was going to make it. If he had gotten to the hospital any later, he certainly would have died. After hours of surgery, the surgeon said he had done all he could do.

I tried to comfort the doctor. I said, "I was praying for my son and for you. God was taking care of you while you were taking care of my Tommy."

Every day when I went to see Tommy at the hospital, I'd pray for him and put holy water on him. Everybody in the hospital thought I was a joke. The doctors said he'd be a vegetable, he'd never be normal. He just lay there while I prayed. I was reading the Bible and saying my rosary. "Dear God, please help us and take care of Tommy and bring him back to us."

A month passed with no change. Then one day, his eyes and left hand moved! I called Father McDonaugh and asked him to pray. As it turned out, Tommy was out of his coma, for two weeks before we knew it. Although he was alert during that time he couldn't talk. He didn't know what had happened or where he was. He could only move his hand a little. He was on a feeding tube for three months in all.

For those three months and every day after, I told everyone that my son would be healed 100%—not 99%, but 100%. I wasn't going to give up. But the truth was, he was still just a vegetable in bed—until one day he started mumbling something. The first word he said was, "Mum, mum." Can you possibly imagine how I felt when I heard that? The second word he said was, "Love." The third thing he said, was "F--- you." That's when we knew that Tommy was back to normal.

The doctors told me I had too much expectation of a person with severe head injuries. I would explain to them, "My son is a special head-injury patient. My son walks with God, and he will be healed."

Tommy knew I was into prayer because I'd taken him and the girls to Father McDonaugh's healing services. The kids would often ask me to pray for them, even though they didn't go to church. After the beating, though, the girls started going to church with me. And driving to the hospital, we'd all say the rosary and pray together.

Every day we'd see signs of improvement in Tommy's

condition. After 3 to 4 months in the hospital, he began to say more words, move his legs, then his arms and by the time he'd been there for 5 months, he was grabbing the nurses. During the next 2 months he started to understand what had happened to him. We kept explaining that he had been beaten, and he'd almost died. We kept telling him, "You're back, pal, whether you like it or not. This is the way it is."

The end of January, five months after he was beaten, I brought Tommy home. The doctors didn't want me to, and I knew it would be a lot of work, but I wanted my son to come home. He returned in a wheelchair, but that didn't last long. Within a few weeks, he went to a walker, then he was down to just using a cane. He was determined to walk.

Seven months after the accident he went to his high school prom. He really couldn't talk much. He was paralyzed on his right side and was wearing a leg brace, but he could still get around. He went with a beautiful girl and all the kids at school were very loving and supportive. Tommy was the king of the prom and he danced with every girl. He never sat down.

To this day our psychiatrist insists that eventually Tommy is going to be violent and angry because of his head injury. Tommy doesn't get angry. Of course we've had our fights, but he's always happy and loving. If he sees anyone in a wheelchair, he'll hug them and touch them. He'll close his eyes and pray for them.

The doctors told me that Tommy was aphasic, which means he's lost the power to use words. When I enrolled Tommy in a head-injury school in September 1991, the doctor thought I was wasting my time. He said Tommy would never be able to read or write.

"Watch me," Tommy answered. "They said I never walk. I never talk. I never read, I never write. I do it all. Move over. I am alive."

Tommy is reading and writing now and he's working on a computer. He can't read the directions, but if you tell him what to do, he'll do it. He's also an artist—he can draw with his left hand. And he can sing any song even though he can't say every word. It doesn't make any sense, but he does it. His speech was basically destroyed and he had to start all over. One day Tommy asked me how he should pray to God. I said, "Just talk to God the way you talk to me. But don't yell at Him."

Every morning I go to Mass and pray that Tommy is taken care of. God probably says, "June's at it again. What does she want today?"

I also call on Michael, Raphael, and Gabriel, the three main angels, every morning and I say, "Will you guys hang out with me today?"

I pray without stopping. I pray when I need a favor, when I'm thinking of my children. When I get up in the morning and exercise on my Stairmaster, I do my rosary. The more I pray, the more I get. I'm addicted to the rosary, and Tommy is my answer to the rosary.

When George, the boy who beat Tommy, was in court, Tommy asked him, "Why?" He said he had no reason, he just wanted to kill someone. The police told us that the boy was on medication for some kind of psychological problem, and was drunk that night.

But our family can't think about hating George. It will just eat away at us. So instead I pray, "Dear God, as much as it hurts, help me to forgive this boy for what he has done to Tommy. Help me to just love."

George's mother (her first name is also June) came up to me in court, and she wanted to talk to me. My daughter said, "Please, Ma, don't. You'll be bringing her back to the house for supper!" And I would because I felt so bad for her. I told her I couldn't talk to her at that time, but someday I would. And I will.

I'm not the best person in the world, but I can't stop talking about God. I love God so much. I'm praying for a miracle. It might not happen tomorrow or next month, but I give Tommy one year and I know he'll be reading and writing perfectly. No one else knows it, but I know it. Tommy knows it. And God knows it.

Two days after I interviewed June Fay, she introduced me to Tommy. He is a somewhat tall, lanky, dark-haired 20-year-old. He put out his hand and said, "I'm Tommy."

His eyes are dark and animated, and as I talked he watched me intently. His responses were slow but understandable. Although his vocabulary was limited, I could see in his eyes that he knew what he wanted to say but he just couldn't dig the words out of his brain. The frustration was hard to watch at times, but I found myself sensing what he wanted to articulate but couldn't.

During a conversation about his attitude concerning his future, Tommy picked up a drinking glass and struggled with several words, one of them being water. His eyes were intense, and he got to his feet to try to pantomime what he couldn't verbalize. He showed me the glass and pointed with his hand that it was almost empty.

"I got it, Tommy," I said. "You don't see a water glass that is half empty, you see it as half full! That's how you see your life. You're an optimist."

"Yes, John. Full, full!" he said, with a big smile I can still see.

From Darkness Into Light

Surely there is no greater gift to a man than that which turns all his aims into parching lips and all life into a fountain.

Kahlil Gibran

John Henry is a 28-year-old survivor of a traumatic and abusive childhood that led to a life of drugs, alcohol, crime and promiscuity. He is now the resident manager for a West Hollywood apartment complex that houses men with AIDS.

I interviewed John in his small, neat apartment. His boyish good looks are common in Hollywood, but he spoke with a maturity beyond his age. Deeply involved in an Alcoholic's Anonymous recovery group, John also thinks about a future that includes teaching, writing, and painting.

My parents had both been married once before they married each other, and they both had children from their previous marriages. Together, they had my brother and me. Dad was a redneck general contractor; a womanizer who was out with the boys every Friday night. My dad, who was abused as a child, was also physically abusive to me. I didn't know my mom so well; she divorced my dad and then committed suicide from a drug overdose when I was two. Three years later, my father gave up my real brother for adoption.

• • •

I remember one time when I was about eight years old, my father handed me a Dr. Seuss book and told me to learn how to read it by six o'clock that night. I sat in my room all day with my Dr. Seuss book and at six, when I couldn't read it, Dad punched me in the mouth and chipped a couple of teeth.

From the time I was seven to ten years of age, one of my stepbrothers molested me. Since it was the first time anyone ever paid any attention to me, I misconstrued it as love.

When I was ten years old, my father started beating me, once with a barbed wire; other times with ropes and switches. I told my schoolteacher what was going on at home and I was put in a foster home for a short time. But then I was returned to my dad's and the abuse from my father and my stepbrother continued, so at the age of 11, I ran away and refused to ever go back home.

The court put me in a boy's home for the next five years. Neighbors took me to church. I had this strong sense of a God, but in my mind I couldn't figure out why, if there was a God, was I going through such pain? Why did my father abuse me? Why was I walking to school crying? Why did I feel powerless?

At 15, I returned to my dad's very briefly. As soon as the abuse started again, I left and stayed with a friend. The courts found me and put me back into the boy's home until I was 18. At the home I started acting sexually with men, just looking to be loved, or accepted.

By the time I graduated from high school, barely, I was an emotionally bankrupt kid with no self-esteem and no skills. I moved to nearby San Bernardino and got a job in a gay bar. That didn't last very long—I couldn't pay my rent because I spent all my money on drugs and alcohol. Eventually, I moved to L.A., where I got a job in a bath house.

By the age of 22 I'd been in jail eight times for check fraud and credit card scams, and I was living in bath houses and on the streets. The only things that mattered to me then were staying high and going dancing at night in gay bars. I was constantly high during that time of my life. I had no sense of self-worth, no confidence, nothing. Humiliated and ashamed, I ended up turning tricks on Santa Monica Boulevard.

One night, walking down Hollywood Boulevard, I realized I had no money, no friends, no drugs, no family to call. I dumped my bag of clothes into a trash can, took off my jewelry and threw it down on the sidewalk—and I asked God for help. I'd already tried everything else. I cried out for God even though I really didn't know who God was. I cried like a wounded animal until I finally fell asleep behind a gas station.

In the morning I went downtown and applied for welfare. Then I went to a shelter to get cleaned up and later to a recovery house where I got sober.

Several months later, I turned myself in to the police for my check scam activities, for which I served eighty days in jail with three years probation.

For the next two and a half years I remained sober and started to turn my life around. I developed a house-sitting business where I took care of wealthy people's homes, paid their bills, oversaw remodeling, and anything else that needed to be done. I had a relationship, two cars and some money—things that made me feel good. But I never really dealt with my emotions. I knew God was there somewhere, but He was kind of off on the sidelines.

I tested HIV positive in 1986. I wasn't surprised I was HIV positive, and I accepted it in the same unquestioning way I'd accepted all the other bad things in my life. Two years later, I received more bad news: I had cancer of the lymph node.

I had the tumor removed, only to discover I also had cancer in my neck. Since I had spent all my savings on the first operation I was sent to the county hospital for treatment. The doctors there gave me only six months to live; I was scared to death. A bunch of tests were run and I was given all kinds of medication, but none of it helped. I underwent painful spinal taps and bone marrow tests but I just got sicker. At this point, my best support system was a man named Jerry, my sponsor from my Alcoholics Anonymous group. A sponsor helps you through the program, and holds your hand when you need it. Jerry did much more than that. He was working on his Science of Mind minister's license. Throughout all of the horrible tests and illness and pain, Jerry stayed with me and prayed with me.

On my ninth morning in the hospital, I woke up with my consciousness changed. I know this was due to my prayers. If I was a being of God, I wasn't supposed to be sick, lying in a hospital dying: I had too many things to accomplish, I had goals and dreams.

At the end of the next day, I went home from the hospital. I returned for chemotherapy treatments once a week for six months. The doctors told me I'd lose my hair and a lot of weight. They said I should quit working and live as stress-free a life as possible. I often thought about losing my hair, dying, being in my grave. But Jerry would always bring me back into the now, force me to focus on prayer. He reminded me that when I prayed, I was praying to a spiritual universe and that my thoughts were in a spiritual realm.

Sometimes I'd say, "God help me to express unconditional love to others today." And other times, I'd giggle—I'd giggle with God! Jerry didn't want me to tell anyone that I had cancer because he didn't want me to get sympathy—or to accept myself as sick.

When I was home, I ate like a pig, and I kept a journal about what was going on inside me. At the top of each page I would write, "God please help me to be honest."

I continued working through the twelve steps of my recovery program, and I made God my best friend. I'd walk around and talk to Him. I'd ride my bike and sing "Amazing Grace" with my own lyrics. And my prayers became prayers of gratitude: I truly believed that everything was going to be okay.

Then at the end of three months, the doctors told me the cancer was in remission.

During that time, I gained a lot of weight and I didn't lose any hair, despite the doctors' predictions that I would lose weight and my hair. And I had more T cells at the end than I'd had before I started the therapy. I'd been given six months to live and nobody—including the doctors—believed the chemotherapy would work except for me. My prayers enabled me to defeat the odds.

In March 1992 I sold everything and moved to Hawaii and then to Spain for four months to regroup, pray, and think. I felt I'd created the cancer, because I was an incredibly angry person. Since I'd ignored the hatred and hostility that had built up during my childhood, I was convinced it had manifested itself through some of this anger as disease.

When I got back to Los Angeles, a friend told me to apply for an apartment manager's job. I manage a low-income apartment house built by local, county, and state funds for people with AIDS; it's a place for them to live in and die in.

This job works my every nerve. I have 26 residents, many of whom are emotionally disturbed. So not only do I have to deal with other people's emotions and suffering, but I must constantly confront my own feelings and reactions. Sometimes I go to bed with so much pain I can only comfort myself with the thought of God's hands holding me.

After the first year, we got more funding so I was given a raise, my hours were reduced and a therapist and a psychotherapist were brought in to train me to do a better job. I also have a beautiful apartment, full medical and dental insurance, and a cat!

And now I have a very full life. I have wonderful friends, I'm helping people who really need me, and I have feelings I've never had before. I'm not on any medication for my HIV nor any special diet. I do my prayer work, I work with the people in the apartment house, and I talk to God a lot. If that doesn't heal me, then I guess I'll be taken to the next step, whatever that may be.

When I'm going through something really scary or challenging, I dig down below all my baggage to God—and he's always there. I still have to fight the concept of a God sitting upstairs in a white coat like my father.

Recently I was doing something—shaving, I think—and all of a sudden I felt like I was in a different realm. I experienced this incredible sense unlike anything I've ever felt before, as if nothing could affect me, nothing could hurt me. I don't know what it was. My instinct was to grab on and hold it but when I started to, it was gone!

A couple of days later when it happened again, I knew that AIDS wasn't going to affect me and the blackness inside me wasn't going to harm me. It was a real sense of being spiritual, a spiritual being having a human experience. I walk around and tell myself that I'm okay, but I know that I have to continue to get rid of my childhood baggage. That's my spiritual job and that's my prayer: I need to clean house so that God can be revealed.

The Miracle Baby

But thou, when thou prayest, enter into thy closet, and when thou hast shut thy door, pray to thy Father which is in secret: and thy Father which seeth in secret shall reward thee openly.

Matthew 6:6

Janet and Bob Steele are married and live in Lake Elsinore, California. Janet, 32 years old, is a nurse and Bob, 31, is a computer operator for a bank. Janet is short and sturdy and has a nurse's no-nonsense attitude towards life. Robert is a lanky, talkative, and thoughtful man who clearly enjoys fatherhood. Their sons are Joshua, 3, and Nathaniel, 5 months. While I was interviewing Bob and Janet, Joshua tried to include us all in his attempts to play with the cat while little Nathaniel lay quietly and happily in his father's arms. Janet and Bob took turns talking about the birth of Nathaniel.

JANET: At around four in the morning I went into labor. I told my husband and then got dressed and drove to the hospital. We decided my husband should stay with Joshua until someone could come over to watch him. As a nurse, I knew I could make the drive alone. It was no big deal since the birth of my first child had been no problem. I told Bob I'd call him when I got to the hospital.

I didn't realize there was a problem until I was actually in the examining room. When they monitored the baby's heart rate I could hear it and I knew it was bad. It was very slow, almost sluggish. The heart would stop and start. The nurses determined I had no amniotic fluid in my uterus, so they started rushing around to give me an amnio infusion, to get fluid around the baby.

I had worked at the hospital for nine years and all the nurses were my friends. They knew right away that I had to have an emergency Caesarean, so they called the doctor and prepared themselves in case the doctor was late.

Everyone knew what to do and I was hoping they could perform the procedure in time. I don't recall anyone ever saying the baby was doing badly, it was an unspoken truth that they all knew. The Caesarean was going to be done right in the delivery room because they didn't have time to move me to an operating room. But while we were waiting for the anesthesiologist, the baby's heart rate picked up a little so they took me to the operating room.

Prior to the delivery, Bob and I had discussed having my tubes tied after the birth, but when the doctor arrived and realized what was happening, he recommended canceling the tubal ligation, "Because this is an emergency and we don't know what's going to happen." In other words, I might want to have another baby so I shouldn't have my tubes tied. I agreed with him.

My background as a nurse in the delivery room helped me. I knew what everyone was doing and why. They didn't have to explain a lot to me. I just signed the papers and let them do the C-section. Getting emotional about it was not going to do anybody any good.

But it kept getting worse.

When they did the Caesarean they discovered the umbilical cord was wrapped around our baby's neck twice, very tightly. The doctor didn't know how long he had been without oxygen. Four minutes without oxygen can produce brain damage; it can start even sooner, depending on the trauma. The baby was limp with no muscle tone so they immediately gave him an IV into his umbilical cord. By now, an hour had passed since I arrived at the hospital.

Shortly thereafter, the baby started having seizures—usually an indication of brain damage. Cutting off oxygen to the brain causes lesions or scar tissue to form: These, in turn, produce seizures. The doctor gave him dopamine to help his kidneys and his blood, phenobarbital for the seizures, and several other drugs. Still, his little arms were rigid, jerking and turning in; this is called posturing, and it's a sign of possible major brain damage.

After a Caesarean operation, a pediatrician always evaluates the condition of the baby on a scale of zero to nine. They consider muscle tone, breathing, response, and so on. A normal baby is rated nine and nine. Nathaniel was a two and four, which is very bad. They gave him a two because he wasn't dead and they had to give him some rating. I found out later he had the worst rating of any baby born that month. The night nursing supervisor called Bob and told him to come right away.

BOB: It was around five in the morning when the nurse called. My first reaction was total shock. As I drove to the hospital I kept thinking about "will"; God's will and my will. I prayed that God knew my heart and He knew that my will was to have a healthy baby. I prayed that He would keep me strong and help me accept whatever was His will.

When I got to the hospital, Janet was unconscious in the recovery room. At that point I was still in a state of shock—I didn't know what to think. I called one of the elders of our church and asked her if they would pray for our baby. We all prayed right away that God would heal him and give us the strength to deal with whatever came our way.

JANET: Bob was made aware of everything that was going on with Nathaniel while I was still unconscious from the anesthesia. There were two nursery nurses in attendance, and one was crying because she knew how bad it was. She wouldn't even go into the delivery room.

After I revived, Bob and I prayed together and separately. We had the church praying for us, his sister and her husband in Hawaii praying for us, as well as our relatives in Nebraska and Michigan. We had a real prayer chain in action.

BOB: When I first saw Nathaniel, he had an IV and a ventilator to help him breathe. He wasn't doing well. His whole body was shaking and his arms were flailing, like one continuous shiver. It was really weird because even though he looked bad, I was confident that God could make things all right. I felt God could do anything and since I had already asked Him for help, it wasn't logical to get angry or throw things. That would be assuming the worst.

I had my Bible with me and I read, mostly by myself. I read passages about how the Lord is your shepherd and He will provide, He is your comforter and will take care of you.

JANET: I was mostly praying, "Please, God, give me the strength to deal with this." We didn't know whether

Nathaniel was going to live or die. And if he did live, we didn't know what kind of condition he would be in. If he wasn't going to be okay, I wanted to still love him, and if he died . . .

• • •

Our community hospital is small and doesn't have a neonatal intensive care unit. I was able to see Nathaniel for only a few minutes before a doctor's assistant took him to the University of Irvine Hospital's intensive care unit about an hour away.

BOB: We can't understand God and His plan. He can take a bad incident and turn it into greater good. We didn't know if Nathan had been brain-damaged or would be seriously handicapped. God's plan might have included us ministering to other people as a result of this incident, perhaps for parents without faith who need someone to talk to.

My prayer was, "God, please make everything all right with Nathaniel. I want you to heal my son and make him healthy and normal. But if that is not your plan and we are to be used in another way, I pray your will be done."

Not too many years ago, I wouldn't have had the maturity to pray that way, because I was too selfish. God's not some great big wishing well in the sky. We have a give-and-take relationship: We learn what it is He wants for us and we accept His will. It's about being humble and letting go of your human desires and acknowledging that God's love for His children is powerful.

• • •

The first day when I went over to the intensive care unit, Nathaniel's breathing was raspy. You could hear the fluid in his lungs. He was still posturing with his arms, which wasn't a good sign. It was difficult, yet at the same time I had an increasing sense of calm and peace about the whole situation, a feeling that it was going to be okay. It was strange, because there was a very good chance that it wasn't going to be all right.

Some elders of our church came to the intensive care ward to pray. All the hospital staff knew they were there. I was confident God was hearing all our prayers and it was going to work out in the long run, even if the result was not what we wanted.

By the second day in intensive care, Nathaniel's seizures and posturing had decreased considerably. Then on the third day he had improved so much, I insisted that Janet's mother come over to see him. She had been almost as worried as we were.

After a week in intensive care at U.C.I.'s hospital, Nathaniel was brought back to our local hospital. The nurses commented that they had never seen such a dramatic improvement in a baby. In one week he had gone from "flatline," seizures, and a dismal prognosis to being called a "miracle baby" by the pediatrican and the nurses.

Jesus said, "Believe I am in the Father and the Father is in me, and if you do not believe for my sake, believe for the sake of the miracles." Miracles are God's way of validating His son. People who would deny that there is any power in prayer have either never experienced it or they're just unwilling to turn to God.

JANET: Prayer is a heart-to-heart talk with God, my almighty Father. He protects me and is with me all the time. I don't pray to get physical or material things. I pray to get closer to God. God doesn't have to be reminded that we exist. We have to be reminded that *He* exists.

BOB: In prayer you open yourself to God communicating with you. Listening to God is as important as praying to Him. Jesus taught us how to pray. He gave us model prayers and commanded us to pray to God, to talk to God, and reminded us that God is good and there is a right and a wrong.

JANET: My spiritual path is improving. The more I learn, the better it gets. If you want to get good at something you have to work at it, so I try to read the Bible and pray every day.

The profound impact of my experience with Nathaniel will never wear off. How could it? You never think such a thing will happen to you. Then when it does, it gives you that much more faith. That's why God performs miracles. Even though He's no longer walking around in the form of Jesus healing people, He does heal. There are miracles.

Every day Bob and I realize how lucky we are. We could be visiting Nathaniel in an institution instead of having a normal, healthy baby at home with us. The doctors, the nurses, and the medicine played an important part in how well he's doing, but you certainly can't disregard God's hand in it. We have a beautiful son. Our prayers were answered.

BOB: There is not a day goes by that I don't look at Nathaniel and think, thank you God, thank you.

Chasing the Rainbow

And be not conformed to this world: but be ye transformed by the renewing of your mind, that ye may prove what is that good, and acceptable, and perfect will of God.

Romans 12:2

Melody and Dwight Lewis were married four months after they met in 1993. Both are in their early 30's and are former prison inmates with histories of cocaine abuse. Melody, who gives motivational speeches about overcoming drug abuse, is a sturdy woman with a laugh that resonates through their immaculate apartment. She is pregnant with their first child.

Dwight has a weight lifter's physique and the face of a leading man. He works at a Los Angeles hospital as a records clerk. Before I began to interview them we all held hands while Dwight prayed for a successful visit and book. They then took turns telling me the stories of their lives.

When I left their San Pedro, California, apartment, Melody gave me a small paper plate of fruit and vegetables to eat on my drive home.

MELODY: In grade school I had a normal, black middle-class life in Los Angeles, going to church and having family outings. Dad was delivering newspapers, which put him in touch with a lot of friendly women. My mother wrote poetry and started hanging out in night clubs with musicians. Eventually, she became a full-fledged alcoholic.

I saw my dad beat my mom a lot. She'd be literally black and blue after the beatings. Throughout high school, our family was pretty much dysfunctional. With all that fighting going on with my parents I felt unwanted and unloved, so I looked for acceptance by other people.

At the age of 13 I became pregnant. My parents found out when I was six months along, and they made me have an abortion. That was the most devastating thing that had ever happened to me. Things didn't get better for a long time.

The kids I hung out with smoked marijuana, snorted cocaine, and drank, so naturally I did too. By the time I got out of high school I had been through so much I wanted to start another life.

DWIGHT: My life began in Los Angeles in 1961, the second youngest of nine kids, all by different fathers. I never knew my father. My mother came from a family of eleven. I grew up in the inner cities of Los Angeles, Baltimore, Newark, Atlanta, and San Bernardino, California.

I started smoking and drinking when I was 13. At 15 I was working for an older brother who was a pimp. Then at 16 I was arrested and jailed in Las Vegas for pimping an older woman I was living with. Later on I was arrested and jailed for stealing a purse. I was also involved in selling drugs, bunco, and credit card scams.

While I was living in Atlanta I was drinking and doing a lot of cocaine until I got so depressed I checked into a mental institution. I was diagnosed as manic depressive and given psychiatric drugs. In 1981 I was diagnosed by another mental institution as schizophrenic and manic depressive, and again I was given drugs for treatment.

After my release, I went back to California. I was arrested in Hollywood for selling crack and went to jail for thirty days.

When I got out of jail a lady I was living with took me to a church in south central Los Angeles. She was interested in religion, and she told me that my life would be better if I accepted Jesus Christ as my savior. The church members laid hands on me, baptized me and enrolled me in the church's religious classes. I didn't really know what I was doing; I just did it for her, I guess.

I didn't change anything about my life over the next few months. I was still living with the same woman and we were both using drugs and drinking. I started beating her pretty often.

MELODY: In high school I had gotten a nursing certificate, so when I graduated I started working as a nurse. My mom knew a lot of musicians and I started hanging around night clubs with her. I also sang at a male strip club. I got pregnant for a second time when I was 20 and had my daughter (she's 14 now). That slowed my night life down a little. But I still found the time to get into trouble.

I was working in a bar when I started snorting cocaine. Then I was introduced to crack cocaine. It's like riding a roller coaster and being at the top. You'll do anything to keep getting high. It's called "chasing the rainbow." I soon became a full-blown addict. One time I did cocaine for 30 straight days.

I prostituted myself to get money for crack, and eventually my Dad threw me out of the house. I slept in parks, alleys, or cars. I had very little confidence in myself. If I didn't have money, I'd trade my body for cocaine.

When you're on the street it's not like being a call girl in a fancy hotel. You're in a car and it's more like, "Let's do it and get it over with so I can get some dope."

I did things I never thought I would do: I was in orgies, I was with several men at a time; I did all sorts of weird sexual things. You reach a point where you do anything for drugs. Drugs completely took over my mind, my life.

I caught walking pneumonia twice from smoking crack. Each time when I got better, the first thing I did was get high. I remember walking down an alley with my crack pipe and praying, "Lord, I don't know why I smoke this stuff." Every time I'd get high I would literally see spirits warring for control of my life.

One night I was in a car with a guy who wanted to touch me, and I wouldn't let him. I think he wanted to rape me. He didn't have money to pay me. I got out of the car, and he hit me in the jaw and knocked me down. When I woke up he was standing over me. I started screaming and all of a sudden out of nowhere this guy with a huge gun showed up. He put me in his car and took me back to my neighborhood. My friends couldn't believe my jaw wasn't broken and that a stranger would help me. I like to think that night there was an angel looking out for me.

DWIGHT: I don't think there were any angels in my life. I went to computer school for a little while, then I quit. I also quit my job as a cook at a catering company, and I went back to hustling on the streets. My woman was selling herself for money. I got mad at her one night for having sex for free with a guy who came to our house to smoke crack. I was delirious and high and I beat her with a belt and a golf club. Then I sodomized her and threw her out of the house.

I was sentenced to eight years in the state penitentiary for bodily injury and sodomy. In prison, I realized I was tired of the life I was living. I had a sister who was a devoted Christian and she encouraged me to change, to really become a Christian instead of just talking about it. A life with the Lord would be better than the one I had, so I rededicated my life to Jesus.

Though I was making progress, I was still smoking and looking at porno magazines. A Christian inmate named Santos talked to me about the music I listened to while I was pumping iron.

"Brother," he said, "that music is worldly and leads you back to Satan."

So I started hanging around Santos and praying. I began attending Bible study classes and soon I realized that prayer was changing me. Jesus went back to the garden of Gethsemane three times. After he got through praying he said, "Not my will but thine be done." I believe the more you pray, the more God aligns you up with his will. I knew that my mind needed to be renewed, so as part of my repentance I wrote a letter of remorse to the woman I had beaten.

I knew that God was changing me because I started helping people instead of hurting them. There were a number of troubled men in prison, and the system doesn't really help them: It just keeps them alive. My friends and I took some of these guys under our wing. We'd cut their fingernails, bathe them, cut their hair, take them to church and get them clean clothes.

And I prayed all the time. This is how I'd pray: "Dear Heavenly Father, I ask you to just touch these men in prison and save them and deliver them. I pray, Father, that you live the life before them that they might see Christ in me. I pray for their families, Lord. I pray that you keep them together. I ask you to touch and help them when they are weak and send other Christians to help them. I pray, Father God, that you protect men from being raped. I pray for people in the streets and I pray, Lord, that you just turn their lives around. Give me understanding of your word and the courage to preach and teach it every day and to live a Christian life. Amen."

• • •

The prison chaplain asked me to be his clerk. I started a prayer circle, learned how to minister to the inmates, and when I was released from prison I went right into a New Testament Baptist Church in Wilmington, California.

I got a temporary job answering phones, then did construction work at an oil refinery for 500 bucks a week. That was the most money I had ever made honestly in my life. I also visited prisons and ministered to jail inmates.

MELODY: In 1987 I served six months in jail as part of a three-year suspended sentence for selling drugs to an undercover police officer. After I got out, I never finished my probation because I was always "dirty" and couldn't pass a drug test. A judge finally sentenced me to three more years due to my parole violations, but there was a typographical error on my transcript and I ended up with a four-year sentence! I wrote to the judge, and even got a lawyer—but the court wouldn't acknowledge their mistake.

While I was in Los Angeles County Jail waiting to transfer to the state women's prison, I read a little book about how somebody came to know God and Jesus. I read a prayer in the book that said, "Lord Jesus, I ask you to come into my heart. I know that I am a sinner. I ask you to have rule over my life right now. I accept you as my Lord and personal savior."

That book did a real job on me. I sat on my bunk and cried and cried until I couldn't cry any more. I looked for more books. I wanted to know more. After that, my life started to change. I started reading the Bible and when I got to the women's prison, I joined Bible classes and started praying every day. Jail was my college to learn more about God.

I was actually glad that I went to jail. I was tired of street life and crack and prostitution. But I was angry that the judge wouldn't admit his sentencing mistake. I cried and cried about it. I was so hurt. "God, how could you allow this to happen? I'm going to church every day, taking classes through the mail, and trying to witness to other women." I was a basket case. But then the word of God brought me out of it. Paul says that no matter what state you are in, you learn to be content.

A lot of women come into prison and want to fit in with the crowd and be cool. Drugs were easy to get: Some women would prostitute themselves with guards to get dope. It's really scary to see how women can be led astray into bad things in prison.

But all I ever did was go to church. I ushered in the church and sang in the choir. I took a lot of Bible classes and was involved with Project Interchange, where I would go out to talk to kids in school. I also got another nursing credential while I was serving time.

People looked up to me because I stayed right there on that straight line. They saw the power of God working in my life, and they knew I had that inner strength. My favorite Psalm was 119, and I read it every night. It was full of wonderful prayers and different ways to be obedient to God. I thought about my ways and God's ways and I turned my feet toward Him and never looked back.

Members from the Greater Ebenezer Missionary Baptist Church in Los Angeles had meetings every month in prison, and I was baptized by them in 1991. They gave me motivation and were the kind of people I wanted to be around. I told them I would come to their church when I got out of there.

When I was released, I realized that even though I had served more time than I should have, God was taking care of me. If I had served a shorter sentence, I probably would have gone back to my old ways. I'd be dead now, praise God.

I eventually went back to my old neighborhood and lived with my dad. Satan tried to set me up many times. The Bible says, "Cast down these vain imaginations." I still get tempted by my imagination. Our minds are the playground for Satan. He knows our weaknesses. Sometimes I see myself hitting the crack pipe again but I also see myself dying on the streets and sleeping in alleys. My brother smokes crack and once he tried to give me his pipe with cocaine in it, but I told him, "I will call the police on you, brother."

Another time, a guy I knew came by in a tricked-up Chevy low rider.

He wanted me to go for a ride.

I just melted. I love old cars. It was newly painted and really cool.

He promised to bring me right back. So I got in and he started racing around the streets. I noticed he had a big gun in his pocket. Then, just as he was showing me some dope he had under the seat, we passed a cop car. I almost died. I could have gone right back to jail just because I went for a ride! This was a warning to me and I learned a big lesson.

• • •

God is in control. I can't do anything without him. That's why I pray all the time. When I meet people I knew when I was on crack, their mouths just drop. I tell them, "What you're looking at is the glory of God. It's nothing I have done to myself." God uses me to glorify Himself. If it wasn't for God's love I would not be standing here.

DWIGHT: In June 1991 I met a Christian woman ten years older than me and we were married. I still didn't know how to treat a woman, and I was dominant and harsh. Instead of trusting God and trying to be obedient and making a successful marriage, I wanted everything my way. She wanted out of the marriage. I ended up completely out of control and I kidnapped her. I was caught and sent back to prison.

Having come so far before this setback, it was a disappointment, but I learned that if any man be in Christ he is a new creature. I repented and confessed my sins and I learned to take responsibility. It wasn't my environment or my upbringing making bad choices; it was me. The Bible says, "If he desires the office of the Bishop, let him be above reproach."

In prison I would prostrate myself on the floor when I prayed. Prayer is just talking to God. When I pray it gives me a good feeling. His presence overwhelms me with joy and happiness. God sees me as His little child and He loves me immeasurably. I know I sometimes break His heart but I also bring joy to Him. Prayer brings me closer to God and it changes me.

I brought my troubles on myself because "as a man soweth, so shall he reap." I believe God allowed many things to happen to me because I had lessons to learn.

I got out of prison on July 23, 1993, after a straight year of time. I still loved my wife but she didn't want anything to do with me.

My prayer for my ex-wife is that someday she will be able to forgive me, go on with her life and keep serving the Lord.

MELODY: As Dwight and I have both learned, there is the darkness and there is the light. Darkness is when you do drugs and are in bondage and do things you never thought you could do. Being in the light, you see the person God truly made you to be and not what Satan wants you to be.

My life today is great. I met Dwight when he gave a talk at our church about how his life had been changed through Christ. We were married four months later. Now we both work in Prison Fellowship and with Straight Talk; we go into high schools and colleges and testify. I also run a drug program on Thursday nights at our church.

I like to go out and tell people the truth about the gospel of Jesus Christ. I'm not proud of my past life, but I'm not ashamed. I'm a child of God and I just keep on praying. The Bible says, "Therefore any man be in Christ is a new creature. Old things are passed away. Behold all things become new." Everything in my life has become new.

DWIGHT: I praise God for the opportunity of preaching in prisons and being able to show inmates that you can live an honest, Christian life without drugs. If an inmate doesn't have God in his life, doesn't have proper guidance and good role models, he will go astray. My desire is to show them you can make it out on the streets. My goal is to become a full-fledged minister with a congregation.

I love people. I love life and God made us to enjoy it. I thank God for blessing me with my wife Melody and for my child that she is carrying. I'll never learn all about God but I know that He is the best thing that ever happened to me. Amen.

Several months after our interview I called Melody, and she happily informed me that she and Dwight are the parents of a healthy baby boy, Dwight, Jr.

The Winding Road

I shall never believe that God plays dice with the world.

Albert Einstein

Peter Profeta was born in Washington, D.C., and raised in Queens and Brooklyn, New York, as well as New Jersey. A former chiropractor, he now lives in Las Vegas, Nevada, where he hosts a daily listener call-in radio program as "Peter C."

I interviewed Peter in his comfortable Las Vegas home. His oil paintings hung in the family room, where several posters and pictures by Jonathan Rogers were also displayed. Peter chain-smoked as we talked, his voice still carrying the accent of his New York roots. He and his wife Carlyn attend the Church of Truth in Christ in Las Vegas. Peter also takes his mother to Catholic Mass on Sunday mornings.

In 1978 I was driving to the Playboy Club in New Jersey to visit a friend who worked there. I had been drinking and was half bagged. There's a stretch on the winding mountain road where the speed limit is 35 miles an hour and if you go 45, your tires are squealing and it's a struggle to stay on the road.

My life wasn't going so well at this point: I was about to get divorced, I was drinking too much, my business wasn't going well, and I was tired of living a life with so many problems. Often during that year, I thought if I had an "accident," I'd spare my family the shame of knowing I committed suicide. As I approached that winding part of the road, I realized this could be the perfect solution. I closed my eyes and floored the accelerator, certain I would die.

But when I opened my eyes, I was somehow through that stretch of the road. I had no idea how I'd made it. I'd been going a lot faster than 45 miles an hour: I should have gone off the road and down the mountain cliffs. God had to have been driving my car because it certainly wasn't me. I was drunk, confused, and scared. It was a miracle I didn't kill myself.

Overwhelmed by the enormity of what had happened, I pulled over to the side of the road where I cried and cried. For some reason, God had stepped in and saved my life, and I hadn't the foggiest idea of why my life had been spared. It was only years later that I realized my dear mother was praying for me almost nonstop during that period of my life.

Prior to the low point, I had led a normal life growing up in a Catholic family on the East Coast. I was in the Army in Korea, where I met and married a Korean woman. After the war, I went to college, then on to business school. After earning an MBA, I went to chiropractic school and started my own practice in 1974 in New Jersey. That's when I started drinking, at first just socially, then gradually increasing until I was drinking every day.

After work I'd always drink from a bottle I kept in the office. Lunch would inevitably include a few martinis. Then when my wife and I started having problems after ten years of marriage, my drinking increased. To compound my misery, I managed to sabotage my professional life as well. I got into a senseless fight with someone who referred me about a million dollars' worth of patients each year. My anger cost me almost my entire business!

At the time, I didn't understand my behavior was typical of an alcoholic enhanced by the attitude of a compulsive gambler. I needed the constant excitement of living on the edge, or my life was boring. Eventually, I sold my practice, split from my wife, and went into hibernation.

I spent most of the next six months writing my autobiography. I'd get up in the morning, have a shot of scotch, make some coffee and start typing. I'd alternate drinking coffee and booze until I was so blitzed I'd stagger into the bedroom and collapse. When I woke up I'd start the process all over again. I seldom left the house or bathed, didn't shave, ate nothing but macaroni and cheese, and drank half gallons of vodka and scotch.

After six months, when I ran out of money, I got a job at McDonald's. I made 200 bucks for a 70-hour work week, and I did it for a year and a half. By 1984, I'd had enough. I started reading the Bible and praying, I stopped drinking, and went back to being a chiropractor. That worked for five years until 1989 when I decided to sell my practice and begin a spiritual quest. Although I was getting by, I wasn't really fulfilled.

I stayed at my home in New Jersey and prayed. "God, I'm searching for the truth. Your truth, not mine. You've got to guide me, lead me. I want *the* truth. Please help me, God."

I concentrated on the four gospels, Matthew, Mark, Luke, and John. I also studied Eastern religions. As I went through various books, I found similar threads of truth in different religions. I realized that if something is true, it's true for everyone.

Every Sunday I went to Mass with my mother. I wasn't really taken with organized religion, but I was comforted by the communion. In my mind it brought me closer to God. I had been raised with a sense of closeness to God, and I'd missed it. Over time, I began feeling more comfortable in my own skin.

My mom sold her house and moved to Las Vegas in 1991. My sister already lived there, so I decided to join them. When I was a chiropractor I used to go to Vegas to gamble and drink, but I always thought I had it under control. It wasn't until I worked with a hypnotherapist (who's now my wife) that I discovered my behavior and feelings were that of an alcoholic. Hypnotherapy led me to go to a few Alcoholics Anonymous meetings, but since I could stop drinking whenever I wanted, I convinced myself I wasn't an alcoholic.

I did realize, however, that I was a compulsive gambler: I was always gambling with my life. After I spoke at a meeting of a Gamblers Anonymous group, a man pulled me aside and said, "You're an alcoholic. Trust me, Peter, I've been there."

For a week after that meeting, I thought and prayed about it. Then I went to an A.A. meeting where a woman stood up and announced that she was a totally functioning alcoholic: She had never lost time from work or been arrested for drunk driving. Her description sounded really familiar. Now that there was a name for it, I realized that I, too, was a functioning alcoholic—as well as a gambler.

Once I'd accepted my condition, I kept on praying and going to meetings. And slowly, my perception of God began to change. The God I'd always prayed to was a vengeful and bloodthirsty one; an old man with a quill and indelible ink, marking down all my sins. I'd always given God human characteristics because that made it easier to perceive Him. But gradually, I began to feel that God was a God of love, and light, and compassion—not a vengeful, judgmental God.

My prayer became very basic. It was as simple as, "Dear God, help me not to gamble with my life today. Help me not to take a drink today."

I began to believe that God saw me as an expression of Himself; His presence was within me. If I allowed God to express Himself through me, then I could do what Jesus promised. "If you believe in me, all the things that I have done, you can do even greater things."

• • •

It got better, but it was never easy. In January 1992 I started a current events talk show on KLAV radio, which was located in a casino. One morning I walked through the casino on my way to work, and I glanced at a crap table. The compulsion to buy chips and throw the dice was overwhelming. It had nothing to do with the game; I don't even know how to play craps. It was the whole feeling of the action, the excitement that I was addicted to: This was the insanity of the disease. After my program, I rushed through the casino with my head down and quickly drove to a Gamblers Anonymous meeting.

The image of myself as a big-shot, hard-drinking gambler with money, fancy clothes, and a big car was part of my addiction. Once I was almost broke but I couldn't bring myself to give up my car. It was too much a part of my identity. (It was repossessed). It was stupid. Now, I'm at a point where my daily prayer is, "Here I am, God. What can I do to serve You today? How can You use me to help a fellow human being?"

Soon I found a way to help lots of people, people who desperately needed help—right in Las Vegas. In November 1993 my wife and I had been doing a lot of praying about my current events radio program. Carlyn thought I should be doing a program about recovery, given the extraordinary number of people in recovery living in Las Vegas. As we continued to pray for the knowledge of God's will and the power to carry it out, Carlyn got the idea that I should do an actual twelve-step recovery program on the air.

January 3, 1994, was our first broadcast of the recovery program. Although we lost some listeners, we gained many more. About the time of the show's launch, our car's engine blew. It would cost $3000—more than we had in our entire savings—to replace it.

We couldn't afford to fix the car, but we desperately needed one. So we started to pray. We prayed and prayed to know that God would provide us with what we really needed, not what we wanted. I was talking to God the way I'm talking to you. "You know the situation, God. What are You playing games for? What am I going to do? Please, I need an answer!"

Suddenly, I had a strong urge to call one of my friends who was also a listener.

She reminded me of a guy I had previously met, the

general manager of the Saturn West Sahara car dealership. I called him and told him my story and he said, "Meet me in my office tomorrow. I think we can help you."

The next morning at the showroom, he told me to pick out any car I wanted. He offered to buy enough advertising time on my program so that I could afford to lease it. (I bought my air time from the station, so all the ad revenue was mine.)

I drove out with a top-of-the-line, fully loaded 1994 Saturn. I choke up even now when I talk about it. I needed a car, and God provided it for me in the most unexpected and wonderful way!

My best reward of all is that the radio program is helping a lot of people and we know we've saved some lives. Listeners tell us they've recognized themselves and their own problems in other callers they've heard talking about their recovery on the air. I know firsthand that the hardest thing for people to do is to admit they have a problem.

In the summer of 1994, all of my prayers were answered. On June 6, I had my last drink. I had heard too many stories in recovery meetings from functioning alcoholics who turned into dysfunctional alcoholics. Then, on July 7, I quit gambling. Now I got to Alcoholics Anonymous meetings two nights each week and another two nights are spent at Gamblers Anonymous meetings.

The twelve-step recovery program is a tool, and our radio program is used as a medium to help addicted people. We don't dwell on how bad it was, we dwell on how good it is. I had a 13-year-old on the program who talked about being free from alcohol and drugs for 100 days. We get letters from out-of-state tourists who say they didn't know they had a problem until they heard our program during a trip to Las Vegas.

We've had calls from people who are going through really difficult periods—and they ask our listeners to pray for them. Later, they'll call back and talk about how the prayers helped them. Our program constantly reminds its listeners about the power of prayer.

Pursuing my spiritual path has been like peeling off the layers of an onion to get to the core of who I really am and what I'm supposed to do with my life. The only reason I'm doing this radio program is that when Carlyn and I prayed, this is what we were shown to do. There was no way I could refuse: I'm either going to turn my will over to God or I'm not. Even when it looks financially bleak, I truly believe I am doing God's will here in Las Vegas.

A Spiritual Astronomer

The starting point of divine Science is that God, Spirit, is All-in-all, and that there is no other might nor Mind—that God is Love, and therefore He is divine Principle.

Mary Baker Eddy

Dr. Laurance Doyle is an astrophysicist with the SETI (Search for Extraterrestrial Intelligence) Institute at the NASA Ames Headquarters, Moffett Field, California. He earned his doctorate in planetary astrophysics with cum laude honors from the University of Heidelberg, Germany, in 1987.

One of a set of triplets born two months prematurely, Dr. Doyle and his brother and sister were not given much of a chance by doctors of being able to survive for a year. His mother became a student of the Christian Science religion, and through prayer alone her babies overcame the medical prediction and survived.

A bearded bachelor, Dr. Doyle wears his hair in a long ponytail. We began our talk at an outdoor cafe on a summer afternoon after he taught Sunday school at a Northern California Church of Christ, Scientist.

I became interested in astronomy when I was three years

old; I got a map of the solar system and I was hooked. I suddenly realized there was a lot more going on than just the planet Earth. By the time I was eight, I was teaching astronomy to all of the neighborhood kids. They'd come over at 6 P.M. and I'd help them to memorize names of the planets with my map of the solar system.

It wasn't until I was 13 that I realized that studying astronomy was an effort to know more about God's creation. Every time I discovered something new about the universe, I realized that looking at the stars was like looking at myself. A Chumash Indian once explained that the purpose of a dolphin is to remind us to have fun and to be joyful. In much the same way, the purpose of astronomy is to remind us that we are not small, that we are unique and invaluable; because in all the immensity of the universe there is only "one each" of us.

When I was about 14 I was struck with the realization that all was *Mind*—one infinite Mind. This concept changed my whole way of thinking: There was only one infinite Mind, and that was what people were really talking about when they talked about God. It's as if your body is in your thought, rather than your thought being in your body. Consequently the Mind of God becomes your thought, your thinking. All the healings I'd ever heard about suddenly made simple and perfect sense. Prayer was letting that Mind which Jesus exemplified be in you. So God doesn't express Himself through us, God expresses Himself *as* us—and I was that idea. This "breakthrough" really put me on the permanent spiritual path.

In high school I had the chance to prove my theory of healing. I was competing in a judo tournament and a guy grabbed my finger and pulled it back until the bone was sticking out. My instructor said it was broken and sent me to the hospital to get it X-rayed. My mom drove me to the emergency room and we sat there for about 45 minutes waiting to see a doctor. In the meantime, I thought about the Bible story where God healed Job when he prayed for his friends. I began talking to and comforting all those people with me in the emergency room until I completely forgot about my hand. When I did look down again, the bone had gone back into place.

When I got my X ray the technician said that the bone had been broken, set, and sealed already—and that I shouldn't have come to the emergency room at all. The evidence of the broken bone was so obvious that it made the healing extra special: Nobody could argue that it hadn't really been broken. My interpretation of the healing was that your hand exists in your thought. So when your thinking is correct, nothing—including time—can stop the healing process. The same mechanism that enables worry to create ulcers turns a positive attitude into good health.

• • •

As a teenager I started to let my hair grow long because I was living near the Navajo reservation and I wanted to participate in their culture. But in my junior year, the principal kicked me out of high school because he thought my hair was inappropriately long. While I was thinking about how to deal with this problem, I turned to the Bible and read the Sermon on the Mount. I read about loving your enemies, blessing them that curse you, and doing good to them that spitefully use you and persecute you. The sermon said, "Love your enemies," so I tried to think of how to be loving. I had a very strong feeling that I should go back to school and let the principal know that I loved him.

There was a lot of social turmoil for kids in those days, and I knew that the principal was under a lot of pressure. So I walked right into his office and told him, "Hey, no hard feelings. I understand you're just doing your job." We ended up talking for four hours and by the end, he was no longer an enemy. He told me I could come back to school and keep my hair long. He also perceived that I desperately wanted to pursue my astronomy career, and he offered to write a recommendation that I skip my junior and senior years and go right to college. My prayers had a powerful impact.

My motivation was not to be clever, and my prayer was not to skip the last two years of school, it was to let the principal know that I loved him and there were no hard feelings. But the outcome proved to me that this prayer is really potent.

And I still believe that the fastest way to grow spiritually is to love your enemies.

• • •

I'm always asked, "How can you be religious, a Christian, and at the same time be a scientist, an astronomer?"

Einstein said, "I want to know what God is thinking." Da Vinci said, "Some people see the ocean, I see forces." In Psalms 147 it says, "God tells the number of the stars. He calls them all by their names."

When I was working on the Voyager Space Project, someone commented to me God must be offended because we were exploring His solar system too thoroughly. "There are 400 billion solar systems in this galaxy," I said, "and there are hundreds of billions of galaxies, and believe me, God would not have created this universe and our ability to explore it if he didn't expect us to do so!"

There is no point to astronomy if it isn't teaching you about the harmony, order, and mind of the creator. To say there is no creator is absurd: It's unthinkable that this universe happened by accident. Can you calculate the number of accidents that happen around you? Creation begs the question! Electrons aren't their own intelligence. Quantum physics isn't the final word.

We used to think the universe was random, then we thought it was a clock; now we know that it's a Mind. Astronomy, physics, and quantum physics help throw off mental limits. Isaac Asimov said, "Science is when you compare your thoughts with those of the universe to see if they match." To me, that is also a definition of prayer.

I don't think you can have a creation separate from a creator, and I don't think you find out more about God by ignoring the universe, by not asking questions. Most of the time when I pray, I kind of throw my thoughts out to the universe. I get quiet and try not to superimpose my preconceptions or my words on Mind. I listen to what the universe, or God, or Mind, is saying to me. To me the key to Christianity is unconditional love and the key to science is unconditional truth. The great breakthrough is that unconditional love and truth are compatible.

I believe that Mary Baker Eddy, who wrote *Science and Health* over one hundred years ago, discovered that reality is perfect. That's what Jesus was demonstrating thousands of years ago. If I had to invent a religion or create a universe I would want an absolutely infinite God that is love and a perfect creation. Jesus said, "Be ye therefore perfect." He didn't say, "Become ye therefore perfect." He expected perfection *now*. So now we are in an age when we're demonstrating that perfect reality.

A prophet in our age doesn't say the Messiah is coming. A prophet in our age says reality is perfect and I can show you. You don't have to ask God to make you perfect; God already loves you so much, all you have to do is accept that.

We are at the verge of being forced by physics into accepting the fact that thought and body cannot be separated. What are the laws of thought? What are the laws of Mind? That's the renaissance. That's what is coming. And that's why I pray.

The Arrow That Flies by Day

> *If all the sons and daughters of the church would know how to be tireless missionaries of the Gospel, a new flowering of holiness and renewal would spring up in this world that thirsts for love and truth.*
>
> *Pope John Paul I*

Fran Fraleigh, a divorced mother of two, lives in Norwalk, Connecticut. As the coordinator for the Catholic Charismatic Renewal movement in the Bridgeport area, she organizes workshops, retreats, and healing prayer services.

Fran is also an active member of St. Philip's Parish in Norwalk and serves as a leader of the church's prayer group.

An attractive blonde in her 40's, Fran wore a stylish black dress to our meeting in her sunny office. Prominently displayed on a bulletin board next to her desk was a three-inch nail, a duplicate of the one that played such an unusual part in her prayer life.

When my interview ended, Fran gave me a card with a religious poem she had written. On the other side of the card was a drawing of a little blonde girl wearing leg braces, sharing an ice cream cone with a Christlike figure.

I was born and raised a good little Catholic girl in a loving family in Norwalk, Connecticut.

During part of my childhood, I had a form of cerebral palsy and I had to wear leg braces and do special leg exercises. Sometimes my parents would reward me with an ice cream cone for doing my exercises. In my mind I'd share my ice cream with Jesus. I always believed in God and I actually planned to become a nun. But after high school, instead of entering a convent, I got a job and then I got married.

Even though I abandoned my plan to become a nun, I didn't abandon my faith. I was active in my parish, and when folk masses became popular, I played my guitar and led the singing. I also taught religious education. Despite my involvement with the church, I felt there was something missing in my Catholic faith, something I couldn't tap into. I couldn't understand why, if you were ill and prayed for a healing, you had to go to a shrine, Lourdes or Fatima or someplace like that, for a miracle.

Although I wanted to have children, I was unable to conceive, so we adopted a baby boy in 1974. In the process of adopting a second child in 1976, I became sick. I was in pain, I had a rash on my face, parts of my body became swollen and eventually I went to the hospital with a temperature of 106°. I was diagnosed with lupus, an incurable skin disease, and I was given megadoses of cortisone steroids to control the condition.

Early on during my treatment, I was invited to bring my guitar to a Catholic charismatic meeting. I sat in the back row, very much a skeptical observer. But I was excited by the vibrant singing, which never occurred at Mass, and I listened intently as some of the people prayed in tongues.

They also talked about what God had done for them; they talked about healing, the holy spirit, and miracles—subjects I'd never heard discussed in church. I heard testimonies that moved my heart.

I thought, "Gee, maybe there's something here for me. Where do I fit in?"

The Catholic charismatic movement, which reaches out to Catholics in an evangelical manner, was only about ten years old in 1976. At the service I attended, I saw it wasn't the usual ritual and quiet prayer. There was more energy—it felt more like a Black church service. People were alive, happy. I was really moved by the service, so I asked for prayer. I thought, "Whatever God wants for me in my life, He'll give it to me."

My prayer was answered a month and a half later when I discovered that I was pregnant! Since I thought I was unable to have children, this was very unexpected. We stopped the adoption proceedings and prepared to have our own child. But along with the excitement there were some complications. Due to the medication I took for my lupus the doctors were very concerned about my pregnancy. It was so serious that we had to discuss the possibility of abortion. I was really confused—overjoyed, but concerned for the health of my baby and myself. I went to the charismatics for more prayer, and ultimately I decided to have the baby.

Every night throughout the pregnancy I'd rock in my rocking chair and cry and pray. Every time I took a pill for my lupus I asked God to bless that awful medicine. I'd say, "God, I'm taking this in obedience to the medical profession but I'm asking you that it not have any negative effect on my baby." My prayer group was praying along with me.

According to my doctors' instructions, I stopped taking my lupus medicine three months before my daughter was born. On March 17, 1977, I gave birth to a beautiful, healthy seven-pound, seven-ounce baby girl.

• • •

After thanking the people in the prayer group for the prayers that gave me my daughter, I asked them for a healing of my lupus. I remember sitting in the prayer circle and thinking I may have a rash, but God is stronger than any rash.

Several months went by and I began to feel stronger and more confident. So I asked my doctor to send me to a lupus clinic in Boston. He agreed and after a series of tests, they couldn't find any trace of lupus.

I went to my prayer group to give them the good news, and to thank them once again.

• • •

Two miracles had occurred in my life: Beyond all expectations, I conceived and gave birth to a healthy baby girl. And, I'd been cured of lupus, a chronic illness. I attribute both of these miracles to prayer and God's love for me. Little did I know that a third miracle was in the offing.

I always had faith, and I had learned that prayer didn't have to be a private thing. I continued attending charismatic services. These services appealed to me because people there were prayed for, not just by priests, but by laity, people like me.

But I still had some questions about their practices.

I went to see my own pastor, as he had had some experience with the charismatic renewal prior to mine. "Why do I have to go outside my parish to have a prayer meeting? Why can't we have one here?" I asked.

He told me to go right ahead, and he put me in charge of starting our local prayer meeting.

In 1978, along with a group of parishioners, I was involved in starting the St. Philips prayer community. We began with, "Let's just get together and praise Jesus and talk about the spirit of God."

I became a prayer leader and worked in music ministry and doing hospital work. My involvement in the prayer community changed my life radically; I went from being a conservative, quiet Catholic woman to someone who was on fire for the Lord.

In 1985, I was appointed charismatic coordinator for the whole diocese in Bridgeport. I was astounded! I was a mother of two with only a high-school education. One of the first things I did was to work on getting more and better office space for me and my staff.

On August 20, 1987, I was sitting at my desk, working on a request for another room. I heard a loud bang, then a bright light came out of my eye and I felt like my brain had exploded. Debris fell on me and I screamed, "Jesus, help me!" A shot, a light, a scream. I was terrified. What happened to me? I grabbed the side of my head and looked up to see a hole in the ceiling. I felt blood coming out of my head and I dropped to the floor.

The vicar general came running in and knelt down beside me. "Fran, I'm going to give you the anointing of the sick."

My brain interpreted that as the last rites, and I became very fearful. Then a man rushed in, a carpenter who had been working upstairs. He was very upset and he explained that he'd been using a nail gun that somehow got loose and he wound up shooting a nail through the floor into my head. I was fading in and out as they were talking. "We can see the point of entry in her skull, but where did the nail go? It's three inches long!" I heard someone say.

I was rushed to the emergency room of St. Vincent's Hospital which, fortunately, is right next door. I was conscious but very confused and afraid.

Madeline, who worked in my office, came with me and held my hand while I waited to be X-rayed. She started singing "On Eagles' Wings:" "And He will raise you up on eagles wings, bear you on the breath of dawn, make you shine like the sun, and hold you in the palm of his hand. You need not fear the terror of night nor the arrow that flies by day. Though thousands fall about you, near you it shall not come. For to His angels He has given a command to guide you in all His ways."

The song just permeated me. I'll always be thankful for Madeline's love for me and her love of God. I recalled the scriptural saying, "Perfect love casteth out fear." I became more peaceful and ready to accept God's will.

The CAT scan showed the three-inch nail hit my head, depressed then fractured my skull, and stopped centimeters from my brain lining. How it came out is still a mystery. It took a long time to find the nail, which was not in my head: It was lying on my desk! When I grabbed my head I must have knocked the nail out.

The doctors didn't know if they should operate on the hole in my head so they put me in intensive neurological care and told me to stay awake all night. They were concerned about neurological damage because I was having some fluttering problems with my eye and trouble with my leg. I talked to my prayer group friends on the phone. The word of God and the promise of healing were all being filtered into my thoughts.

My daughter asked me, "Are you going to die, Mommy?"

I told her I didn't know.

"Well, I love you," she said.

And I found myself saying, "I love you, too."

The doctors took a second CAT scan because they expected more problems. I'd gone through all the prayer and singing with my friends and now this? I was angry and started crying. But my bed was surrounded by my friends, my prayer partners. God would not let me alone. He had all these people praying for me and encouraging me.

And by the next day, the hole in my head started closing up. The doctors in the hospital would stop to look in at the woman who was shot in the head with a nail. And every time they did, I'd give them a message of hope. I used the experience to help the faith of others.

On the fourth day the doctors must have figured the Lord was definitely with me, because they sent me home.

While recuperating I had to deal with thoughts of "why me?" Sometimes I was unable to pray because of my anger, but people from all over the country prayed for me. Whenever I felt a peace in my heart due to their prayers, I was able to say, "Lord, here I am. I'm yours. I know you didn't send me that nail." That's the old Catholic guilt trip. But I know that God was not punishing me.

I struggled tremendously with headaches and just not being able to do ordinary things. I asked God to give me a forgiving heart towards the man who shot me. I knew it had been an accident.

I used the experience as a time of grace, a time to pray. I couldn't read very well because of the pain, but I spoke to God from my heart. I prayed in everyday words. "Here

I am, Lord. I am your servant. You are greater than this. I feel so helpless. Please heal me."

When I was recuperating in pain and confusion in my bed, people would call and ask me to pray for them. I did, and my friends were blessed and healed. Why lie in bed and complain? Others had worse problems than I did.

The doctors didn't give me any medicine, as my body was pretty much allergic to most medications.

When I returned to the hospital for checkups and CAT scans, the doctors were amazed and pleased that I was healing so quickly. I think God intervened.

• • •

To believe in miracles doesn't mean you have to go to a shrine. You can pray for a miracle in your living room. God is everywhere. God wants to answer prayer. I don't think people realize that.

God wants me to come to him not out of fear and damnation. He doesn't want me to be programmed to show up every Sunday in church. God doesn't want me to come to him for a reward. He wants me to love Him. I can do that while I'm cleaning the toilet. I can pray or sing any time of the day or night. The spirit of Christ is always drawing me to God.

People today have so many needs, but psychiatrists, therapists, and doctors can only go so far. They can't fulfill our spiritual needs. I know what it's like to be afraid, to face death, but I also know what God can do and has done for me. I know that God answers prayers and that God heals.

If I die tomorrow, God's work goes on. What I accomplish in my life doesn't matter—what matters is that I do properly what God asks me to do. It's not my work I'm doing, it's God's work.

Close to the Edge

The steps of a good man are ordered by the Lord: and he delighteth in his way.

Though he fall, he shall not be utterly cast down: for the Lord upholdeth him with his hand.

Psalms 37:23–24

Thirty-eight-year-old Robert Buckley lives in Novato, California, an hour north of San Francisco. A graduate of the College of Marin and the University of California at Berkeley, he has a bachelor's and a master's degree. He and his wife Linda have four children ranging in age from eight years to three months. A banker with a close physical resemblance to Dan Quayle, Bob, dressed in a pin-striped suit, white shirt, and wing tip shoes, was quiet and thoughtful as he talked to me in his small office overlooking the bustle of downtown San Francisco.

At the conclusion of the interview, we walked to a nearby outdoor cafe and had lunch under a beautifully clear, sunny sky. Bob said he was teaching his children to pray and that recently his three-year-old daughter wanted to pray for the chicken they were eating for dinner.

My parents divorced when I was 12. After that, my seven brothers and sisters and I stopped going to the Catholic

Church and I sort of drifted. Throughout grammar school, I was a tough guy with a chip on my shoulder. Then in the sixth grade, I got busted for smoking pot. Around the same time, my cousin and my older brother Mark freaked out on drugs and ended up in the Napa, California State Mental Hospital. The seriousness of their problem really scared me, so I started to pull back.

By the time I was a freshman in high school, Mark had gotten out of Napa and was going to Bible study classes with a group of hippies. I liked hanging with my brother, so I just tagged along.

But pretty soon, I realized something spiritual was going on in the classes and I committed myself to them as much as a 14-year-old kid can. I read the King James version of the Bible all the way through. It was way over my head, but I just motored through it. And I prayed a lot. I felt like I was connecting with something solid—a feeling I'd never experienced going to Mass.

This was in the 70's and at that time, the "hippy way" of being a Jesus freak was pretty confrontational. It didn't make me the most popular guy in school to be handing out religious tracts and calling people sinners. Later I learned to soft-pedal my beliefs because I realized most kids just weren't interested in repenting for their sins.

But I always believed that God had something to say, and I really wanted Him to speak to me. There was one very special time when I came close. My brother Mark and I were praying and talking to God at a Northern California lake. I knew He was everywhere—in the forest, the rocks, and the lake. That was the first time I really sensed His presence, His love.

• • •

When I was 17, three of my brothers and a cousin and I decided we were going to drive down to Mexico via Arizona to surf. When we got to Blythe, California, it was 120 degrees outside so we took a side trip to the Colorado River for a swim.

I put some flippers on and dove off a steep, sandy bank into the water. But the flippers caused me to misjudge my dive—I dove short, landing on the top of my head in about three feet of water.

God did that hurt! I wasn't numb or paralyzed—but my neck was in a lot of pain. I didn't want to be wimpy, but I told my brother John I wanted a neck brace to hold it still and give it support. The drugstore in town didn't have one, so we were directed to a clinic. The doctor at the clinic told us he'd have to examine me before he'd give me a neck brace. They strapped me down and took X rays of my neck.

The doctor brought the X rays to my bed and the guys all gathered around him while he examined them. He pointed to different spots on the X rays while he explained that my neck was broken in five places. The X rays showed the top vertebrae in my neck were pressed together and fractured. He showed it to everybody. My cousin said, "Bob, you're not going to play football this year."

My brother Barry rode with me in the ambulance to Loma Linda University Medical Center, a hospital near Los Angeles that specializes in neurosurgery. The X rays showing the compression fracture were sent with me. I didn't really appreciate what had happened to me until I got to the hospital. The guy next to me in the intensive care ward told me that neck injuries can cause paralysis.

I hadn't realized how serious my injury was—his comment really scared me.

I was immobilized in bed with my head in traction and heavy weights were attached to a head brace by a chain. The doctor said I was either going to be on my back in traction for six weeks or I would get a body cast and a halo with bolts in my skull. Those were my choices.

My brother Mark and my mom came down from Northern California and my other brothers and my cousin drove from Blythe to the hospital. They all went out for dinner except Mark, who stayed with me. I was afraid and I hurt. We both began to pray.

Mark and I just talked to God. I was praying for all I was worth. We both spoke out loud to God and asked for a healing. I think my inspiration came from knowing who God is, how powerful He is, and how much He loved me.

I thought back to the time when Mark and I prayed together by that lake in Northern California. I wanted to tap into that strong, pure feeling.

During this prayer, I felt like God said to me, "You're okay."

It wasn't a voice I heard, it was just a sense that He was giving me a message. I asked myself, "If you pray for a healing and then God says you're okay, what more do you want?" And I had complete faith that He would heal me.

I told my brother to unhook all the traction stuff. I had to ask him two or three times because he was hesitant to do it.

Finally, I explained to him, "I think Jesus or God is telling me that I'm okay." That was enough for Mark.

He walked to the head of the bed and unhooked the chain that connected the weights. Then he took off the noose from around my neck. I immediately started to feel a lot better. I was overcome by a peaceful sensation. Then it got interesting.

My mother came back from dinner and thought we'd gone crazy. She was upset. Then a doctor came in and gave us a bit of a hard time. "I really wish you hadn't done this," he said, "but if this is what you want we'll take some X rays."

X rays were taken, and the technician went away for a long time. Then he came back and told us he didn't get the spot he was supposed to get, so he'd need to take more X rays. There was no longer any evidence of a fracture. That night I slept without a neck brace or traction.

The chaplain came by to see me and said, "Sometimes God heals gradually and sometimes he heals dramatically."

My hospital medical record states that when I was admitted to Loma Linda, "X rays brought from Blythe show a compression fracture of C6 with possible fracture dislocation at C4-5 with offset of about 2mm." In other words there was one and possibly a second fracture, and my neck was out of joint. The Loma Linda doctor's discharge summary stated that after "a healing session" an X ray was taken that "showed satisfactory alignment of the cervical spine" and "no evidence of fracture."

I was released from the hospital the next day, a happy 17-year-old with a Styrofoam neck brace going home three days after he dove headfirst into the Colorado River.

I checked in at the Kaiser hospital at home and got another neck X ray. My doctor there said to come back in two weeks and to continue wearing the neck brace. But I was a wild kid so instead I tore out a lawn at my mom's house plus worked out for football, doing wind sprints and strenuous physical stuff. I wore the brace on and off.

After two weeks my doctor showed me the X ray he took and said, "Well, I see some kind of gray area on your neck X ray. Your records indicate you had a problem, but I can't find anything wrong."

The football coach made me get a physical from the team doctor, and my grandmother sent me to an orthopedic surgeon friend of hers. Despite the fact that I'd had multiple fractures only weeks earlier, they couldn't find anything wrong with my neck.

• • •

I think there is a spiritual force in the universe that looks out for everybody. I also think a lot of people know about this force—and it's not just people who go to church. Ordinary people on the street, the homeless say, "God bless you" when you give 'em a buck. God talks to those who are really close to the edge—people who need Him the most. I got pretty close to that edge and I really believe a miracle happened at that point. God did something for me.

• • •

God is telling me, "Robert, you may think there is a lot of B.S. around here in this world, but good stuff is going on, too. I'm doing good things here." I know that I'm not supposed to be governed by fear, so I really expect the best.

I believe in the biblical definition of God that says God is love. I pray every day, which for me means I basically just talk and listen to God. I usually do this on the bus to work. I'll give you an example of one of my conversations with God.

"God, I know that right now I'm sort of giving a demo

prayer, but I want to thank you for bringing this man John into my office today. Even though I have certain fears about praying in public, I feel you are doing something through John and I'm glad to be a part of it. Also I want to pray for the people in my office, which is something I do frequently. I pray that I have the opportunity to tell them about this interview and that something good will come out of it as well. God, I know that you are not limited to any particular church and I know, Lord, you reach out and touch people in all areas and different nationalities in different ways. Amen."

The Christmas Tree Experience

God answers sharp and sudden some prayers, And thrust the thing we have prayed for in our face, a gauntlet with a gift in't.

Elizabeth Barrett Browning

Sue Michaels was born in Clarksburg, West Virginia, "fifty some years ago," graduated from West Virginia University, and taught school in Maryland. She also had her own antique business in Georgia. She now lives in Ponce Inlet, Florida. I interviewed Sue at the International New Thought Alliance's Transformational Expo in San Antonio, Texas. The theme of the five-day meeting was "Expanding Spirituality as Co-Creators."

Sue, a friendly and energetic woman, told me how watching an Academy Award–winning movie forced her to face her drinking problem.

I started drinking beer when I was sixteen. At first, I drank for peer acceptance. Eight years later, I just couldn't stop.

My parents were both alcoholics, in spite of our family's church background. And growing up in a dysfunctional family made me into a caretaker, always wanting to smooth things over but ignoring the real problems. Dad would disappear for a month at a time on a binge. His alcoholism seriously affected the whole family.

In 1964 I was in my 30's, married, and very active in the Methodist Church. I thought I was controlling my drinking, but I always had several glasses of sherry before going to choir practice, a no-no in the Methodist Church. At the time my husband and I had been trying to start a family, but I was never able to carry a baby for more than a few months. Over the years I had a total of seven miscarriages due to a genetic disorder, and I desperately wanted children.

This was a very painful period for me. Despite several attempts to quit drinking, I always wound up numbing myself with alcohol. There was always the hope that if my husband just stopped drinking, then everything would work itself out. It was always "if, if, if." I would continually wait for him to supply my happiness and my purpose in life. Burdening someone else in this way is the most selfish thing you can do, but at the time, I didn't know it was wrong. As dependent as I was on him, I never knew what he was going to do or say. I was already very emotionally insecure because of coming from an alcoholic family. We had many drunken arguments, some with loaded guns. And often when I went to sleep at night, I didn't know if I was going to wake up the next morning. It was a living hell.

In 1968 I quit my job as a schoolteacher because it interfered with my drinking, and I opened an antique store so I could drink anytime I wanted. If I had a hangover I opened late, and I closed early if I wanted to drink. I'd given up on church and started hiding out in business, drinking and hoping my husband would change so I could change.

After all my miscarriages, we decided to try to adopt a baby. But when we were screened by a psychiatrist, the doctor quickly figured out that I drank too much, was dependent on my husband, and thought a child would save our marriage. We weren't allowed to adopt.

That was the breaking point for me and God. I lost all my faith in prayer because whatever I asked God for was denied me. I didn't realize why at the time.

By 1970, I hit my low point. We were both drunk all the time, but I was convinced that only he had the drinking problem. *The Days of Wine and Roses* led me to get help. In the movie Jack Lemmon plays a drunk and his wife, played by Piper Laurie, begins drinking to keep him company. Eventually he gets help through an Alcoholics Anonymous recovery program while she ends up on the streets. I watched the movie on video several times but I was always drunk before it ended. Then one night, my husband took my bottle away and said I couldn't have it back until I watched the whole movie. He said, "If we don't get help, we're both going to end up like that." So we went to a twelve-step recovery meeting to prove that I didn't belong there. I'd never been arrested for drunk driving. I had never been institutionalized, hadn't lost my home or my job. Yes, I had been turned down for adoption but that was my husband's fault, not mine.

Within the first three months, the group urged me to stop identifying with my husband's and my father's drinking and to identify instead with myself and my problems. This was a big step, because denial was a substantial part of my problem. I blamed my husband, I blamed God—

but I never took responsibility myself.

The first time anyone in my recovery group said that God was love, I was shocked. If there was a God it was a vengeful, hurting God, one I certainly wasn't going to pray to. Hearing that God was love was the door-opener for me.

I looked to the group because they had something I wanted, a heartfelt joy. And they were giving me unconditional love, something I'd never had. They said I should learn to pray to God, however I perceived Him. I was looking to other people rather than to God for support because the God I was raised with was not a loving God. Though as a child I prayed and had spiritual aspirations, well-meaning teachers, parents, and even ministers quashed my hopes with hellfire-and-damnation sermons.

The first prayer I ever really spoke with sincerity was, "God, if there is a God, and I don't think there is, if you can hear me, which I don't think you can, Help!"

I'd forsaken the vengeful God I'd been brought up with and was developing my concept of a God that loved me.

It wasn't until after I was active in the recovery program and had stopped drinking that I began to seriously pray.

• • •

After eighteen months of sobriety, my husband slipped in 1973. Shortly after his first setback, he got drunk a second time during a one-night stand with another woman. I was absolutely devastated.

I was so low, I thought I was going to commit murder and/or suicide. I wasn't sure which. I went to a group meeting really just to say good-bye to all my friends. After our meeting in the church basement, I went upstairs to the sanctuary, to be alone and to say good-bye to God. I was tired of hurting and hoping. Despite my sobriety, I was smoking four packs of cigarettes a day and I was taking Valium as well. I couldn't face life without love and without hope.

No sooner had I started to pray when Gil, a man in the recovery group whom I hadn't seen for six months, walked into the sanctuary. He said to me, "I just had to come to this meeting tonight." Gil was an accountant and an amateur astrologer, so at one time I gave him information so he could make an astrological chart for me. Though we had never had the chance to discuss my chart, he had done his own reading of the situation.

"Sue, whatever you're thinking of doing tonight, don't do it."

"Excuse me?" I stammered.

"This is the lowest part of your life, Sue. I want you to remember that never again will things be this bad. Things are going to go up from now on. Soon you'll have the freedom that you need in your personal life."

At that moment I realized that God manifests Himself through people and that He was operating through Gil, who came out of nowhere when I desperately needed help. It was a big time, a major interjection in my life, and ultimately, this confirmation of God, coupled with the message of hope, saved me.

"You have no idea how you have changed my life," I told him.

Gil smiled and said, "Yes I do."

When I arrived home that night, my husband stared at me and said, "What in the world has happened to you?" He told me I was absolutely radiant—that I looked like a Christmas tree. I felt like a Christmas tree all covered with glistening, colorful lights—a symbol of life and joy, and most importantly, hope.

In 1974 my husband and I were divorced. Basically I told him, "I love you and bless you but I cannot live with you." I also quit a seven-year habit of taking Valium. Two years later, in my third year of sobriety, I also quit smoking. Alcohol, cigarettes, and Valium were crutches, and I didn't need them to get through life anymore because I was learning about God's love for me and the hope that goes along with that love.

It wasn't always easy, though. One night, shortly after my divorce, I was painting the woodwork in the house, trying to keep busy because I was depressed and wanted a drink very, very badly. I knew that if I got in my car I couldn't trust myself as to where I would go. I started talking to God. and I picked up the paint brush dripping with chartreuse paint, threw it at the white ceiling, and yelled, "If you're so damn smart, God, you take it."

At that very minute the phone rang. It was some friends from my twelve-step program calling to chat.

"I need to go to a meeting badly," I said. They told me they'd meet me there.

"I can't get into my car. I'm afraid. Please come and get me," I pleaded.

My prayer that night was from the heart. It was about giving up and being open. I was hurting too much to call, but the phone rang for me. My friends took me to a meeting, and it was just the right place for me to be and the right people were there for me to talk to.

When the student is ready, the teacher will appear. My teachers appeared in the form of all of those experiences. I learned to talk to God. God's our best friend, our Father.

Tell Him what's in your heart. If you have a problem, just say, "Father, this is what's going on. I don't know what to do. I need some insight. Please take it and show me what to do." God doesn't need our prayers. We need our prayers!

My prayers are simple and direct. "Help me, God." I've learned to say, "Thank you, Father," which to me, is a prayer in itself. My favorite prayer is the serenity prayer: "God, give us grace to accept with serenity the things that cannot be changed, courage to change the things which should be changed, and the wisdom to distinguish the one from the other."

I no longer bargain with God, and I know not to ask for the world. God is not loving, God is Love. God is not forgiving, because God doesn't judge. God is not wise, He is Wisdom. You can't put the infinite in finite terms. That's why people have to have God come in a form. The American Indian talks about mother earth, father sky. We want to have imperfect people who become perfect, like Jesus, Krishna, Mohammed, and Buddha. They show us that through them, the divine qualities of God can be expressed.

We are all children of God, and it's up to each of us to develop that relationship. The Buddhists call it the void, Indians call it the great spirit, others call it absolute. It's that inner knowing in all of us that's greater than us.

Meditation goes along with prayer, as far as I'm concerned. Meditation is about being silent, calming down the human in order to hear the divine. Prayer is talking to God, and meditation is listening.

The way I look at things, there is only one truth. There has to be a cause in the universe and that cause, God, has to be the source for everything. We all have our own individual spiritual roads. It's up to each one of us to get to the top of the mountain where we are all one.

It didn't dawn on me until about six months ago that I've overcome everything I've ever been afraid of in life. And all of these fears have been overcome through God's will.

I teach yogic meditation now. After twenty-four years of sobriety I still attend twelve-step meetings to be of service to God and to reach out to love those who need help. In the words of Jesus, the master teacher, "Doing unto the least of these, you do unto me."

Be Careful What You Pray For

Your vision will become clear only when you can look into your own heart. Who looks outside, dreams. Who looks inside, awakens.

Carl Jung

Elizabeth Jaeger is an actress, wife, acting teacher, and a former Miss USA beauty pageant contestant from Pelican Rapids, Minnesota. She is typical of the many young women who flock to Hollywood from all across America in search of an acting career. I interviewed Elizabeth in the spacious Studio City, California, condominium that she shares with her second husband, Derek, a singer, scriptwriter, and actor.

A beautiful woman with a wholesome, down-to-earth manner, Elizabeth often laughed at herself as she shared with me some of the trials and tribulations of her life in Hollywood.

I was so shy as a young girl that I wouldn't even raise my hand in class to talk. But as soon as my braces came off in high school, everything changed. I became a cheerleader, I was homecoming queen, president of the student council, and gymnastics captain, and, as a classic overachiever, I got great grades.

While I was at Moorhead State University in Minnesota, I participated in seven national beauty pageants and I was in the top five at the Miss USA Pageant. Knowing that only one girl out of fifty could win, I'd pray to release my fears about not winning in order to enjoy the pageants. I would say the 23rd Psalm or a quote from Norman Vincent Peale over and over like a mantra to comfort me.

After graduating from college—the first in my family to do so—I moved to Minneapolis to launch my career. I got lots of modeling jobs, did some TV commercials, and acted in plays. But after a year and a half I'd done everything I could in Minneapolis, so in 1988 I moved to Hollywood.

Soon after moving, I married a North Dakota businessman I'd been dating and I started commuting back and forth to be with him.

I quickly learned that it's easy to go astray in Hollywood. The brighter-eyed you look—and I was literally right out of the Minnesota cornfields—the more you attract men who claim to be producers, or agents, or casting directors.

Fortunately, I also met a lot of quality people who helped steer me clear of the hustlers, and over time I had a degree of success. I had small parts in a few feature films in addition to doing a number of commercials and modeling jobs.

But in an effort to propel my career, I had some uncomfortable relationships. I began to realize I had to be someone's date to be in his movie. All the traps of Hollywood—money, drugs, sex, power—fight your inner voice that warns you, "No, this isn't right." If you're desperate—and a lot of people are—you can get really far off the track. I gradually drifted into an unfocused life.

To recapture a sense of purpose, I decided to go on a church search with the girl I was rooming with in Hollywood. We visited numerous churches, went to lectures, and read books. Then one Sunday we went to a Religious Science Church. A woman sang an old Elvis song, "In the Garden," about "when He walks with me and talks with me." But she said "She" in place of "He." My heart seemed to swell up and I cried because I felt she was singing to me about the inner voice of God—which is dwelling in all of us. This was a much more personal vision than the traditional picture of a God somewhere up in the clouds. I had found my church.

• • •

In the spring of 1990 I started having panic attacks. I'd get dizzy, my vision would sort of close in, and I'd have heart palpitations. I could be talking to people during an attack, but it wouldn't really register. I was full of fear about life. Finally, I went to a therapist who concluded pretty quickly what I already knew: "You want a divorce."

To acknowledge that was very difficult. I'd been devastated by my parents' divorce when I was in grade school. Also, divorce was sinful and horrible to me. But I knew that we'd married too young and we were both inexperienced in dealing maturely with the demands of marriage.

When we separated, I crashed. Without question, I went through the worst period of my life. I relived the trauma of my parents' divorce. Those old memories were never healed, and I felt just dead inside. I also realized that most of my relationships were unhealthy because I allowed people to dominate me like I was a little girl. There were days when I couldn't even get out of bed because the feelings of failure were so overwhelming. I could hardly stand up, much less stand up for myself. It was hard for me to go out on acting or modeling interviews. I really believed that dying would be easier than living.

I hadn't asked my husband for any money and I was completely broke, sharing a two-bedroom apartment with five people. I had a girlfriend who worked on a phone sex line, a job I considered before deciding go-go dancing would be better. I wore a bikini, served customers beer, and danced on a stage for money. I didn't like the environment and quit after a few weeks.

Although the turmoil of the divorce, my unemployment, and panic attacks made this the lowest point of my life, my misery ultimately became a catalyst for spiritual growth. I learned how to pray affirmatively through the Religious Science Church. At first, it was scary because as a kid I'd been taught to pray for *things*—to ask this power outside myself to give me what I wanted. Now I was praying to affirm a harmonious universe working for my good. I'd type in prayers on my computer over and over again to convince myself that I was going to be okay.

Instead of praying, "God, give me peace of mind," I'd say, "God, I know I am perfect in peace of mind because I am made in your image and likeness and you are the perfect peace of mind that surpasses all human understanding."

I memorized a lot of Scriptures. I love "Prove me now herewith, sayeth the Lord of hosts, and I will open up the windows of heaven and pour forth a blessing too great for you to receive." What that meant to me was "prove me in the life you have right *now*." It's not "prove me when you get to be a star." It's not that you're going to see God when you have children, or when you have a great career. The Scripture is a challenge to me, from God: "Right now, if you can prove me, accept life for how magnificent it really is, then I will pour forth a blessing too great for you to receive. I will open the windows of heaven and pour it onto you."

In my own way, I accepted that challenge. Over a period of several years of doing affirmative prayers, meditating, reading spiritual material and the Bible daily, going to church three or four times a week, joining the choir and working with a spiritual practitioner, my life gradually changed.

The first dramatic evidence of this change presented itself to me in August 1991. I was teaching at an acting school then; my friends were all there, and the job was my identity. During a staff meeting my boss lied to me—a manipulative, obvious lie—and then, in front of everyone, he turned to me and said "Isn't that right, Elizabeth?" I turned to a good friend and asked him, "Aren't you going to say anything?"

He just said, "No. I think he's right,"

I knew he'd said so to save his job, and so did everyone else in the room. I looked to another friend who just sat there mute. It was just me and God. But at that moment, I realized we were enough. I got up and walked out, knowing I would never, ever return.

Just as my divorce was incredibly hard on me, leaving this job in this way was really tough. I was getting out of another unhealthy, dominating relationship. I was 29, divorced, living with five actors. I'd left my life in Minnesota, and now I'd lost my place in the environment that was the closest thing I had to a family.

But in the same way my "crash" forced me into self-discovery, led me to discover that I was created in God's image and likeness.

I learned through my study and prayer that being "born into sin"—a phrase I was raised on—means being born into limiting thoughts and perceptions of who you really are. My "sins" were my negative thoughts: "Hollywood's a tough town, lots of actors don't make it . . ."

Now I believe in the plan Spirit has for me. Spirit is a term I use as a more generic definition of God or Universal Intelligence; it doesn't have a limiting connotation. Now, my prayers acknowledge that I have a peaceful, loving existence with creative opportunities and joy. That's the truth I accept for myself, and that's exactly what appears in my life now.

I love acting and I love to teach it. It's completely fulfilling, and I know I'm in alignment with what Spirit has in mind for me. In my teaching I pray, "Spirit, send me students for my own growth as well as for theirs." This prayer has been answered with wonderful students that enriched me and my classes.

I used to picture myself as a movie star, but I don't really desire that anymore. I think most of our neuroses and sinful thoughts stem from our attempts to control our lives. But if we just "let go and let God," our lives will unfold naturally and happily.

Years ago, if I didn't get a part I'd say, "They gave the job to that stupid girl who isn't even a good actress!" Clearly, this wasn't a very positive thought or prayer.

When I lose a role now, my prayer is, "I know that the perfect person got the role. I know that Spirit is shining a light through her. She is the vessel to carry it, and in no way does this limit my creative opportunities." I say these prayers until I believe them.

If our thoughts are negative—"This is a terrible, lacking universe. It's a hard life"—they will be reflected in our experience. At the same time, positive thoughts and prayers will be realized. I have proof in my own life that prayers are answered. So be careful of what you pray for! It's better to have a prayer that affirms that I am at perfect peace with myself and my life's path under God's direction.

Things have completely changed for me in the last four years, and it's the direct result of a lot of prayer and spiritual study. I pray, "Spirit, I know you have in your design for my life perfect creative opportunity where I can earn my living in joy." Since I've been praying that prayer, I've had acting jobs coming out of my ears; and students have come out of thin air, it seems, because I don't advertise.

My husband Derek and I are both on a spiritual path, and I never dreamed marriage could be so good. A year ago, when we married, we were financially broke but spiritually rich. Derek wrote a beautiful song for me as my wedding present, and I painted a picture of our relationship for him. Our friends and family presented us with flowers and gifts and things that we couldn't afford. God was just pouring his gifts on us. And it hasn't stopped!

One Cigarette Won't Hurt

God, give us grace to accept with serenity the things that cannot be changed, courage to change the things which should be changed, and the wisdom to distinguish the one from the other.

Reinhold Niebuhr

Ruth Weigers was born in Chicago, Illinois, of parents who were very active in the Congregational Church. She graduated from Arrington Heights High School in 1945. Married for 18 years, Ruth is a divorced mother of six children. Retired, she now lives in Chandler, Arizona. She calls herself a "child of the universe," due to her interest in a variety of religious groups including Unity and Religious Science, two churches that actively use prayer for healing.

Ruth has short blonde hair and a youthful enthusiasm. I took her to be in her late 50's and she laughed when I told her and said, "You're about ten years off, John, but thanks!"

Although Ruth talked about her problems with alcohol, fighting her 30-year addiction to nicotine, she said, was the major challenge in her life.

I started smoking cigarettes when I was 16 years old after

my mother died. It was very "cool" and "in" to smoke in those days. Later in my 20's, I tried to stop smoking but I just couldn't quit. I married an alcoholic, and for a time I developed my own problems with alcohol as well.

Though I was never physiologically addicted to alcohol, the habitual use of it was very damaging. My husband drank himself out of a job at Boeing and was a classic alcoholic as well as a chronic gambler. I got job after job to keep things together for our family—I had six kids in seven years—while my unemployed husband was home drinking all the time. I worked in a freight office for a while, then in real estate, then, interestingly enough, I had a job in the aversion conditioning treatment center of a local hospital. It was run by a recovering alcoholic.

Over the years, my husband tried a number of alcohol treatment programs, all unsuccessful. In 1968 he wrecked a car—the "last straw" that eventually led to our divorce. Since I was the only one employed, I was held responsible by the court for all the bills he had run up while we were married.

I was ordered to pay both attorneys, pay off my own back child support, which he never paid, and then split what was left with my husband. I hired a new attorney, a woman, who filed bankruptcy for me as well as filing a quitclaim deed to the house. I ended up with all the bills, and my ex-husband got married the day after our divorce was final. I was given custody of the children who were aged 9 to 17 at the time.

During the divorce, sometime in 1969, I started praying. But I didn't really know how to do it. I would essentially say, "God, you gotta get me out of this mess!"

I didn't want the kids to hear me crying at night so I

would get in my car and drive down the freeway just screaming and yelling at God to help me. Oddly enough, I felt the most support from the recovering alcoholics at the hospital treatment center where I worked. They were a tremendous help to me.

I also read from a wonderful book, *The Greatest Thing in the World*, by Henry Drummond, who writes about the power of love. At that point I was driving forty miles to work every day, and often I would concentrate on one statement from that book all the way to the hospital. One of my favorites was Drummond's statement, "Is life not full of opportunities for learning Love? Every man and woman every day has a thousand of them. The world is not a playground; it is a schoolroom. Life is not a holiday, but an education. And the one eternal lesson for us all is how much better we can love."

All of this prayer and reading led me to the amazing discovery that by focusing on the knowledge that there is a supreme being, I could dilute my fear. I learned that your mind cannot simultaneously hold two opposing thoughts. You can't be faithful and fearful at the same time. Armed with this insight, I began to feel better about myself.

In the morning I would lie in bed and think about God. I would actually say in my mind, "Good morning, God. We have another day and I know you'll see me through it."

I'd picture this light moving in and through me, dissipating all the anger and frustration in me. I felt that the light was God and if there was anything that was bothering me I would say, God, I need some help with these bills. But my life was still a mess. I was trying to raise six kids, pay off debts, work, and figure out what God and me were all about.

I'd survived the divorce—but I had many challenges ahead. Since I'd never considered myself an alcoholic, I gradually started drinking until eventually I was drinking five or six nights a week. Not the passing-out type of drinking, but enough to cloud my mind and my vision. I was also chain-smoking three packs of cigarettes a day.

One Saturday in 1970 I drank so much that I couldn't drive home. I didn't want my kids to see me that way so I stayed at a friend's house. In the morning I looked in the mirror and said, "Ruth, you know what's going to happen to you if you don't stop this." I'd eventually cross the line: alcohol would turn from a psychological addiction into a physiological addiction. I knew I would die from alcohol or I'd lose my kids if I didn't stop drinking.

I drove home, called A.A. for help, and I haven't had a drink in over 20 years. My growing belief in prayer, the fear of being an alcoholic, and the support from A.A. members all contributed to my recovery.

Another major challenge successfully met, I desperately wanted to stop smoking. Unfortunately, I had a harder time giving up cigarettes than drinking. I was smoking three packs a day and had been for over 30 years. I had tried numerous ways to stop smoking, and none of them had worked. I was completely hooked on nicotine.

At this point, I was really into conversing with God. I begged Him, "Okay, God, tell me about this smoking." The answer I got was that I wanted to smoke more than I wanted to quit.

My prayers had led me to A.A. for alcohol. It became clear to me that I could use their twelve-step program to quit smoking because it was also an addiction.

On the 4th of July, 1972—I'll never forget that date—I went to an A.A. recovery meeting. Coincidentally, the man speaking that night was talking about how he quit smoking! That was my message. God just had it all perfectly arranged for me. So I did what the speaker did. I made a list of all the advantages of not smoking. I knew I was spending a lot of money on cigarettes and that I had a bad cough. My house curtains were discolored from smoke, my clothes and breath smelled of tobacco, my fingers were stained, and I couldn't taste the food I ate. Plus the kids really wanted me to stop. And I knew God didn't want me to smoke either.

I concentrated all my prayers on asking God to help me stop smoking. I didn't just want to quit—I wanted to not want to smoke cigarettes. My prayer life was geared towards quitting smoking on the weekend of August 1. Each day I'd say, "God, these are the things I want in my life. You and I both know that the first step is for me to not smoke. I want you to help me. Please, God help me. I know you love me. I'm ready to do your will."

The evening of July 31 I smoked what I considered my final cigarette and put the three left over from my pack on the fireplace mantle in the living room. The next morning as I left for work, I looked at the cigarettes on the mantle and I asked myself, "Do I want to take those with me?"

"No, God doesn't want me to smoke and I am not going to smoke," I assured myself.

At work there was a lot of pressure and tension in the office.

I kept telling myself, "Nothing and no one is going to provoke me into smoking."

My kids knew what I was doing and were very supportive. But after I put them all to bed, I was almost in tears so I took a bath to try to relax. Conflicting voices kept going through my mind: "I want a cigarette. I have to smoke." "No, don't do it!" "One cigarette won't hurt. Just one." It was truly traumatic for me.

Finally, I fell into bed and burst into tears, praying in desperation, "God, I can't handle this, but You can. Take this from me. Please, please, dear God, release me from cigarettes."

When I woke up in the morning I felt incredibly good. I looked in the mirror and saw an unusual calmness in my face. I went into the living room and saw the three cigarettes on the fireplace mantle. Surprisingly, I didn't want one. I had no interest in the cigarettes. It was shocking and great!

As I went through the day, I felt an intense inner joy. One moment I would believe it, then the next I would say to myself, "No, this can't be happening after thirty years!" Finally I realized that it was true; I really felt God's presence within me and I knew I was free from my addiction to smoking. Sometime during the previous night all my inner conflict had been healed and released. I know that it was God's universal healing presence that saved me and I firmly believe that presence is within us all.

• • •

About a year after I stopped smoking I realized that the sky was bluer, the grass was greener, and flowers were brighter. It was incredible. I don't know if my vision improved because I stopped smoking, or drinking, or both, but it was great. And I could actually taste the food I ate!

I think the entire universe is spiritual and a lot of us just haven't really connected or identified with that presence. When I prayed to be free of the tobacco habit, I was getting myself, the human, out of the way for the divine, the spiritual. The key is that love, God's love, heals. And when prayer is voiced, we are ready to receive the "peace that passeth all understanding."

When I pray—which I do numerous times during the day—I'm communicating on a conscious level with the power and creative presence in the universe. To me, God is that creative presence and is forever creating, sharing, loving. There are probably half a dozen times every day that I see the beauty and love of this universe and say, "Thank you, God. Thank you."

David and Goliath

It's been a long time since the trouble began.
I've watched as my boy has turned into a man,
inside a jail cell, away from us all.
Why won't they listen to this mother's call?
I'm calling people across this great land,
to rise and fight for an innocent man.

song written by Joyce Milgaard

Joyce Milgaard lives in Kanata, Ontario, Canada. She and her husband Lorne have four children, ages 33 to 42. Joyce, a gracious and soft-spoken Christian Science nurse, told me that in 1969 her son David, 16, was—like many restless youths at that time—using drugs and living a free and easy life. All this changed in the summer of 1969 with a knock on the front door of the Milgaard home. When Joyce opened the door, she began an incredible journey that ended 23 years and 46 weeks later in the Supreme Court of Canada.

A small sign on Joyce's desk in her home reminds her of the journey. It says, "Do the Impossible."

The policeman at the door told us that our son David was suspected of raping and murdering Gail Miller, a 20-year-old nurse from Saskatoon. I was shocked and started to cry. The girl was found January 31 lying frozen in the snow alongside a road. She had been raped and brutally stabbed twelve times. I knew David, and although his lifestyle was not what I would have chosen, there was not a vicious bone in my son's body.

When I talked to David in jail he said, "Mum, I know nothing about it. I wasn't there. I never met that girl." I believed him. David and several of his friends were in Saskatoon looking for a guy named Shorty Cadrain so they could borrow money from him. They got lost and made several stops trying to find his house. During this time Gail Miller was killed.

At the trial several people who'd been with David at that time claimed he had blood on his trousers and had bragged about the killing. We believed in our son's innocence and trusted the system. But somehow, David was pronounced guilty. I was stunned. You can't be convicted when you're innocent! And David wasn't even put on the stand to tell his story.

I stood there in court and watched my young, scared son being taken to prison for life for a murder and rape I knew he didn't commit. I felt as if I was encased in ice.

• • •

David had a difficult time in prison. He tried to commit suicide twice. Once he was in solitary confinement for three months and refused to see me. I knew something was wrong, so I insisted on visiting him. Even though there had never been a woman in solitary, I was allowed into David's cell. He looked like an old man. His eyes were glazed, he was stooped, and his hair was matted. He said, "Mum, is that you? No, it's just another vision." I reached out to God and said, "Dear Father, please help me, help him." Immediately David recognized me and put his arms around me and we both cried. The next day he was alert and clean.

I was praying and leaning on God throughout all of our problems. Ever since I had joined the Christian Science Church in 1964, my faith in God's power had steadily increased. I still draw strength from daily studying the Bible and *Science and Health* (our textbook that helps me understand the Bible). I particularly identified with the story of David and Goliath. Goliath seemed invincible but I knew, like the biblical David, that with God, all things are possible. I was made in God's image and likeness and God was pouring forth all the patience, resourcefulness, and understanding I needed. I had only to use it.

• • •

Our final appeal for a new trial was turned down in 1971. In 1975 David escaped from the maximum security prison in New Brunswick. He was only free for a few days; then he was badly beaten by the guards when he was returned to prison. In 1980 David escaped again and was free for 77 days. Being a fugitive wouldn't prove his innocence, so I tried to convince him to surrender, but he refused. The police set a trap for him and when David discovered it, he ran. They caught him and shot him in the back when he was lying on the ground. After recuperating in the hospital, he went back to prison.

Over the years, my entire family was imprisoned in a sense. My kids would come home bruised and crying from fights with their classmates. "Your brother is a killer" was a common taunt. Conversations would stop when I walked into a store. I thought a lot about the crucifixion and how people are moved to do things in a mob that they'd never do on their own.

A woman in my church told me that if I was a good Christian Scientist, my son wouldn't be in jail. I was stunned by her remark, but my strong reaction told me there was something inside me that needed to be healed. I was inspired to read the Bible story about Shadrach, Meshack, and Abednego in the fiery furnace. King Nebuchaadnezzar forced them into the furnace because they wouldn't worship his golden image. A figure appeared in the fire next to the three boys and they were unharmed. I'd read this story a hundred times before, but I suddenly realized these boys were in the fire so the King could see the Christ, the power of God in that situation.

I started to cry because I realized that unconsciously I'd been blaming myself for the fact that David was in prison. Then I saw that my "fiery furnace" experience was also going to prove God's allness, that He was in control—not me. A huge load was lifted off my back. I was actually grateful for that woman's remark because it led me to pray and uncover my own misconception about God. This realization—that God was with me and that He had a purpose for our fight to prove David's innocence—was a major turning point for me.

• • •

In 1980 my family decided to use our pension money and offer a $10,000 reward for information about the case. (At times I was working three jobs at once to help support our family and save money for David's defense). Our reward attracted the attention of journalist Peter Carlyle-Gordge, who'd spent a number of years writing about David's innocence. We also went back to Saskatoon and made a video of David's travel route during the time of the murder. The video proved that it was impossible, according to sworn testimony about David's activities that day, for him to be the killer.

But we needed more evidence. I was continually looking for leads, hitting dead ends, getting my hopes up. In many cases, I found that the police had told witnesses not to talk to us. Throughout what felt like an impossible struggle, I'd pray every day for the strength and courage to continue fighting for David. One time while I was praying, I was just hit by the statement "Rise in the strength of Spirit to resist all that is unlike God, Good" from *Science and Health*. At that point, I had no strength to rise. Then I realized, " 'Rise in the strength of *Spirit,*' not 'Rise in *your* strength'." So I did!

It took eight long and very strenuous years, but by 1988, we presented the court with new evidence—including tests proving the semen found at the murder scene was not David's. We asked that the case be reopened. Despite our compelling argument, two more years passed and nothing was done. We discovered our petition had been ignored and filed. So we kept on pressuring the court. Through all the years of fighting to get my son out of prison, my prayer was, "Thy will be done." I knew that He was working His purpose out, no matter what the human picture presented. I prayed to know what God's purpose was: "God, what are you seeing? What's the truth here? Not *my* truth, but *your* truth?" It reminded me that when I saw a beautifully embroidered rose, the reverse side was a tangle of knots. I often felt my life was a tangle but I knew that God saw the beautiful and perfect side, the rose side.

• • •

In February 1990, one of our lawyers, Hersh Wolch, received an anonymous phone call claiming that Larry

Fisher murdered Gail Miller. I recognized his name. Fisher had been living with Shorty Cadrain, the man David was looking for on the day of the murder. Incredibly, Fisher was already in jail for the rape of several other women in Saskatoon. Based on this lead, an investigator, Paul Henderson, and I spent three months tracking down Fisher's other victims—including a woman accosted by him the morning of the murder.

In May 1990, the Minister of Justice, Kim Campbell, was in a Winnipeg hotel to give a speech. I approached her in the hallway of the hotel to tell her I had new information on my son's innocence and I wanted to meet with her. In the presence of TV cameras, Campbell physically brushed me aside and said, "Madame, if you want a fair hearing, don't talk to me!" When this exchange was shown on TV, every mother in Canada was outraged over the way I had been treated!

A few days later, the thought came to me to write a song to Campbell. I'd never written a song, but the thought of doing it wouldn't leave my head. So for one night, God wouldn't let me sleep, and I wrote a song.

The song complete, I called David Aspel, one of our lawyers who donated his time to help us, and told him that if I couldn't talk to Campbell I'd sing to her. It turned out that just the night before, David had been elected president of the Winnipeg Folk Festival. The musicians at the Festival knew he represented David and told him they wanted to do something to help our cause.

A few days later, I was in a Toronto recording studio with my song and a room full of musicians. Suddenly the studio door opened to let in several TV crews, newspaper and radio reporters. (Somebody had called them and told them what we were doing.) I took a deep breath and said to myself, "Okay, Father, sing this for me." This is part of what I sang:

Please Madame Minister, listen to me.
Please Madame Minister, set David free.
He is not guilty, you have the proof.
How can you stand there, so cold and aloof?
How many people must tell you so?
How many years until you let him go?
Please Madame Minister, listen to me.
Please Madame Minister, set David free.

My song—in reality my prayer—caught Canada's attention. It was on TV and the radio, and it was written about in newspapers all over the country. God wrote that song—the song that turned the tide for us—and it was the result of my prayers. It was God's expression of harmony through me, and it led to wonderful opportunities to prove that God's law, not human law, is supreme.

Unfortunately, human will was still imposing obstacles in David's life. In February 1990, the Minister of Justice turned down our application to reopen David's case. Her decision was a shock. David was very discouraged—he even encouraged me to give up: "You've wasted your life helping me."

I said, "No, David, even if you weren't my son, this is not justice. There is God's justice and God's laws." From that point on, I was working for all the David Milgaards of the world.

The decision not to reopen the case brought more people over to our side. The Anglican and the United Churches, the Mennonites, and the Salvation Army had prayer days for David; sisters in convents held special masses; people sent us money; and the power of prayer spanned all religious beliefs. We created a circle of love that transcended personal differences. One woman called me and said, "I'm praying for you even though you're a Christian Scientist."

The Bible is full of examples of God working through people, showing them that when they do right, when they're honest, right wins. God was there for Peter when he needed to get out of prison. So when I prayed, I steadfastly refused to accept that there was another power opposed to God. I wasn't praying to make something go away; I was affirming what God stood for—justice and truth—which is the real law.

On September 8, 1991, I talked to the Prime Minister of Canada, Brian Mulrooney, outside a hotel in Winnipeg where I was holding a vigil with some of my supporters. In front of the TV cameras, I asked him to help me, and he said he'd "look into the matter."

A month later, after a lot of prayer, I was led to go to Ottawa to call on the Prime Minister. First, I told his aide that I was going to the House of Commons and that I knew the press would want to know what the Prime Minister had done to help me. Within the hour I received a letter signed by the Prime Minister, promising to address our case.

On November 29, 1991, Kim Campbell announced that the Supreme Court of Canada would review David's case. But we weren't allowed to discuss police misconduct. (When the police decided that David, a hippy kid from another town, was the killer, they coerced his companions into lying about his involvement. Then much later, when information about Larry Fisher's past rapes surfaced, the police never informed us or the court.) So our lawyer, Hersh Wolch, presented the case that Fisher was the killer. Testimony from Fisher's ex-wife and prison inmates substantiated our claim. Plus, all of the witnesses in David's car on the day of the murder told the Court that they'd lied about David's involvement during the initial trial.

On April 14, 1992, the Supreme Court decided that David should get a new trial and he should be released from prison immediately. Twenty-two years and 46 weeks after David was wrongfully sent to prison, he became a free man. It was the first time in Canadian history that the Supreme Court had not upheld a conviction.

The Saskatoon court that originally convicted David, faced with all the new evidence and with the public support of David, declined to retry the case.

We have initiated a lawsuit against the police and the government. We're asking them to seek the truth about who killed Gail Miller, and to compensate David for his 22 years of incarceration. The Bible says, "Ye shall know the Truth and the Truth shall make you free." I am convinced this is going to happen.

• • •

David had a rough road but he's doing much better now. He doesn't like to be indoors so he spends most of his time outside. He'll be happier when all the facts of the case are revealed publicly and he is completely exonerated.

I've become involved with the Association in Defense of the Wrongly Convicted. I'm spearheading a movement to change the justice system to prevent a recurrence of what David endured. Our case has attracted many people to the Association, and I'm grateful I can be involved in this worthy cause.

The experience has made me much stronger in my belief in prayer. For all of those horrible years, I was comforted by the first line in *Science and Health*, "To those leaning on the sustaining infinite, today is big with blessings." It gave me strength to know each day—regardless of the Goliathlike challenges I faced—that I could start fresh and "big with blessings." The Bible says it so well: "Now is the accepted time. Now is the day of salvation."

I have learned so much. I have skills I never had before, and I have understanding and compassion for others that I never had. I have been so blessed.

Celebration of the Soul

I learned that days told stories and messages blew through the night wind. God had wings and I could see within them. There was an apple in God's eye and I was inside the apple.

Meinrad Craighead
The Litany of the Great River

Meinrad Craighead is a 58-year-old artist and writer who lives in Albuquerque, New Mexico. Born in Little Rock, Arkansas, she attended Catholic schools in Chicago and received a Master of Fine Arts degree from the University of Wisconsin. Meinrad, who is named after a 7th-century Swiss hermit, spent 14 years as a nun in an English Benedictine monastery.

We sat on the porch of her home next to her studio, which she built herself over the course of two-years. Meinrad is a tall, commanding woman with a direct gaze. I could easily envision her as a pioneer woman, driving a covered wagon across the plains. A soft breeze rustled the trees in her yard, and Meinrad's dog napped at her feet while we talked. My interview began with her questioning me.

"These people that you've interviewed, John, who tell you these wonderful stories about a threshold conversion, an awareness of this God within, does that change their life? Do they really allow God into their life, into the unity of creation?"

I don't have dramatic stories to tell you. In fact, among the wide circle of friends with whom I've had spiritual relationships over the years, I've been considered an oddball because my prayer and my painting is one activity. You can see where my soul is by looking at my paintings. My creative life, my prayer and spiritual life have never been disconnected.

For me, prayer is not crisis-oriented and it never has been. I've never had a great illness. My mother and father died naturally. If prayer is only crisis-oriented, I don't feel it's nurturing. The daily understanding and praying out of our wholeness, as an act of thanksgiving, builds a deep resource; so that when you do have a crisis, it isn't something that breaks your life apart.

I remember one time when I was six years old I stared into the eyes of my dog. I saw a deep infinity in her eyes and I heard within my child's body the sound of rushing water. That infinity and that sound was truly an ecstatic experience for me. I knew somehow that both were definitions of the Godhead. And I understood that it was God as my mother, roaring in my soul through the water.

That deep interior knowing was to be the pattern of my entire existence. Hearing that rushing water inside my body, I named it "mother," mother water. And knowing that She was my source and She had the depth of my allegiance (no matter what layers were on top of it, including the Catholic church), enabled me to understand, in a secret part of my soul, that God was my mother.

On another level, I took in all the poetry and Scripture of the Catholic church. I prayed to God our Father, prayed to Our Lady, as the Mother of Jesus. But through my experience as a child, I named God as my mother. That has been the founding emotional drama of my life, although it wasn't a crisis. It was a gift I was given on a hot sleepy Arkansas afternoon, when I had gone to the north side of my grandmother's porch to get cool.

• • •

Although I grew up poor, I never felt a lack of material wealth. My life was filled with loving relationships in an extended family. At the time, I gave thanks to God because my life was filled with love.

My definition of prayer is an act of thanksgiving for being interconnected with all of life. As human beings, we are only one little piece of the whole, and without the rest, we simply can't exist. This interdependence is part of the divine order, the divine blessing, the divine grace of the cosmos that is being held in the divine arms of the creator.

• • •

When I was 29 I was living in Spain on a Fulbright scholarship and it became clear to me that I was supposed to go to a monastery. This idea evolved through my prayer life—I needed more and more solitude, and a deeper commitment to God, whom I knew wanted me for Herself.

The 14 years I spent in a Benedictine abbey were very productive physically, spiritually, and intellectually. The rule of St. Benedict, which goes back to the 6th Century, is a life wonderfully balanced between work and prayer. Five times a day the great bell in the tower was rung and we all came to pray, whether we were digging potatoes or washing clothes. We prayed what's called the divine hours—the divine office—a ceremony which dates back to medieval times.

Each office is based on chanting the Psalms: "Out of the depths I have cried onto you, oh Lord. Lord, hear my voice. Reach down into my soul, oh Lord. Comfort my afflictions."

What most Christians do once a week for an hour or so, we did for half an hour, five times a day, every day. I loved monastic life. They were good years, happy years. But I had a very, very deep intuition that I was supposed to leave the monastery. It was difficult for me because I didn't want to leave, but it became clear that I needed to tell my own story about my relationship to God as my mother in a series of paintings and writings. To do this, I felt I had to be part of the world instead of being with seventy women in a monastery.

I make paintings because God made me an artist. I feel that I give to society as an artist. I think artists—true artists—feel an enormous responsibility if they have talent. My paintings are my primordial acts of thanksgiving to the Godhead, to the creative spirit living in me and the world. All of the arts are a path to healing.

When people view my work, I hope they fall into the world of their own dreams, into the world of poetry that may come from their children's mouths—or into the sheer joy of creation.

Although I left the monastery in 1980, I didn't leave the church. I've incorporated the ritual that has always been so important to me into my daily life. For instance, my first act when I get up in the morning before the first light is to ritually, very slowly drink a glass of water. When I do this, I feel the cosmic waters flowing into me, as a gift.

You may question the value of a gift that comes out of my kitchen faucet. But to me, it's all part of creation, part of the rains coming down and the rivers flowing and the clouds going around. And during my ritual act of receiving, I'm giving thanks.

In the winter I do a fire ritual in the studio, for practical, organic purposes. This is the Fire God who's going to make my body comfortable so I can work. It's a very simple ceremony. I light a bit of paper and a few twigs and move in a circle around my fire. Everything awakens to light. And as I do this, I pray. I also walk to the Rio Grande River, which is a few minutes away. This physical river reflects the river of life that I know flows from God's throne.

I'm always conscious of the power of water and fire, the organic unity of all creation. I also respect the rhythm of the sun and the moon, and its relationship to the beauty of grain, which comes out of the earth, and turns into bread and feeds our bodies and then goes back into the earth again.

Catholicism taught me ritual. I grew up when the Church was still using incense and the priests wore elaborate vestments. The candles, the music, the liturgy, just fell right into my soul. It's an enormous loss for this generation that the church has cut out most of that ritual. I need ritual every day the way I need oxygen.

There is no prayer without listening because listening means having your ear open to the rhythms, sounds, forces, and energies of the universe. This is where God is. God isn't up in a steeple. God is all around us. The energy of the Godhead could not possibly be contained in any narrow doctrine, whether it's Catholic, Muslim, Jewish, or fundamentalist. The world is full of stories about God. They are like rivers flowing from one reservoir.

Many people have trouble with the organized church, and so do I. Any kind of institution can cripple spirituality. But I'm grateful for my experience in the Catholic church because it taught me the first poetry in my life. But I don't need that structure anymore. I don't need fences to walk along anymore. Many people do need fences; they can't wander in the desert worrying about where they're going. They need a guarantee: If you follow this fence you'll get to heaven, or paradise, or the promised land, or wherever.

So many people move through their lives unconsciously. You should have a conversation with your soul on a daily basis and prayer should be as natural as breathing. Until you know your soul and celebrate your spirit, you are not in full relationship with the rest of creation. Until you are giving back, exhaling God's spirit within you out into the world, do you think you have any right to be here?

If you have a comment about this book or would like to share your own story about prayer, you may write to the author, John Holmstrom, c/o Perigee Books, The Berkley Publishing Group, 200 Madison Avenue, New York, New York, 10016.